Dear Uncle Joel,

I love our friendship & relationship. Thanks for all the years! Looking forward to new summits together!

THE STEADY CLIMB

THE STEADY CLIMB

A Family Journey From
Mountains to Markets

by Jay Hack

WITH MARK SPRINGER

www.hackwealthmanagement.com

ISBN 978-0-692-46334-5 (hardcover)
ISBN 978-0-692-46335-2 (ebook)

Jay N. Hack, MBA, CFP®
Senior Vice President, Investments
Hack Wealth Management of
Raymond James and Associates
31500 Northwestern Highway, Suite 150
Farmington Hills, MI 48334

The opinions expressed herein are not necessarily those of Raymond James & Associates, Inc., member New York Stock Exchange/SIPC. Past performance does not guarantee future results. Information is provided as a hypothetical example. Results may not be typical for all investors. There is no assurance the trends described in this book will continue. The market value of securities fluctuates and you may incur a profit or a loss. Investments are subject to market risk, including the possibility of losing one's entire investment. Diversification and strategic asset allocation do not ensure a profit or protect against a loss. The process of rebalancing an investment portfolio may carry tax consequences. Raymond James & Associates, Inc., makes a market in Coca-Cola, Dow Chemical, General Electric & IBM.

Front cover photo: Organ Pipe Peaks, Antarctica. Photo by Dylan Taylor © 2015
Back cover photo: Dylan Taylor © 2012
Author photo: Ksenija Savic Photography © 2015
Jacket and book design by Give Creative Co.

FOR MY MOM

*A book about our family
wouldn't be complete without
you as the starting point.*

NOBODY RINGS A BELL AT THE
TOP OR BOTTOM OF A MARKET.

— *Wall Street proverb*

REACHING THE SUMMIT IS
ONLY HALF THE CLIMB.

—*Mountaineering proverb*

FOREWORD

INTRODUCTION

R etrospect is a wonderful mechanism for examining one's past accomplishments and subsequently experiencing pride. However, retrospect pales in comparison to hearing the phrase "Dad I want to write a book about what I've learned from you and your career." To have your child validate the achievements that others have commemorated with plaques, awards and testimonials takes pride to a whole new level.

As I was reading *The Steady Climb*, it occurred to me that Jay has expanded the reach of my wealth management philosophy far beyond my original professional goals. Over the past 46 years, my ability to assist people in achieving their financial objectives was limited to those with whom I had direct contact. Now, anyone who reads this book can potentially benefit from what my clients have learned through experience. This also is a special point of pride.

Investors always want to know what the stock market will do in the future. No one can predict that, but, to borrow a line attributed to J. P. Morgan, we can be pretty sure the best forecast is: "it will fluctuate." *The Steady Climb* addresses historical fluctuations and investors' reactions to those fluctuations. By looking back on what investors did right and wrong at critical points in the stock market cycle, readers can gain insight into the emotional extremes and psychological biases that often lead to people to make inappropriate decisions at inopportune times. I believe the mistakes are the stories that have the most to teach us. Everyone can relate to being troubled by fear during a bear market or tempted by greed during a bull market, but rarely do we have an opportunity to step back and examine how these emotions can affect the success or failure of our long-term financial plans.

This book is a wonderful reference source. Read it and put it on the shelf. When you find yourself considering a radical change to your investment posture in the middle of a frightening drop in stock values or a thrilling period of growth, take the book down and re-read the appropriate section. Consider where you are in the course of your own wealth management journey, and consider how the philosophy described in these pages applies to your situation and your financial goals. If you are still uncomfortable with your investments, call your financial advisor and schedule a meeting to talk about your concerns. Use what you've learned here to guide your discussion, and keep the lines of communication open with your financial advisor. If you do that, and if you remain committed to doing what is fundamentally correct in the long term, my guess is the decision you come to will be better than the one you would have made otherwise.

BIRMINGHAM, MI
2015

THE STEADY CLIMB

INTRODUCTION:
From Mountains to Markets

t was raining in the desert when I decided to give up my career as a mountain guide. I'd like to say I made the decision intending to become a financial advisor so that I could go into business with my dad, because that would be a great storyline—son returns from mountain top, joins family business to pursue new heights of success!—but in truth, I never imagined things would work out the way they have. I didn't even know I was on the verge of such a personally significant decision until I made it. I'd just finished a difficult but rewarding three-week stint that included 14 days guiding rock climbing in Joshua Tree, California, a weekend guiding clients in Red Rock Canyon, Nevada, and four days climbing with Mike, a friend who also worked for the guide service.

(Mike and I would often push our technical and physical limits on Red Rock's iconic sandstone cliffs when we weren't being hired to guide.) I was totally spent after all this, and at the end of the last day it was all I could do to crawl into my tent before falling asleep.

I don't know exactly when the rain started, only that I awoke the next morning cold and damp and still exhausted. Fog shrouded the campground, which quickly emptied as the springtime tourists packed up and beat a hasty retreat to Las Vegas. Soon Mike was gone, too, headed home to recharge before going on another climbing trip. Gusting winds kicked up and the morning fog disappeared, blown away in tatters.

I lingered alone in the campground. The North Cascades were my next destination, where I would work for a week or two on Mount Baker in Washington State to prepare for leading summertime expeditions on Denali in Alaska, but I was in no hurry to hit the road. It was a 20-hour drive from Red Rock Canyon to the Cascades, and I knew what awaited me there: more rain, more wind, more cold. And snow. Lots of snow. (Believe me when I tell you it's possible to spend an amazing amount of time soaked on Mount Baker in April and May. This is great preparation for Alaska, but not the sort of thing most people do for fun.) As I sat in the Nevada desert with the wind blowing the rain sideways against my tent, I realized I wasn't looking forward to it.

Guiding in North America tends to be a migratory profession, and for me it was exactly that. I didn't have an apartment or a place to call home, just my tent and my Jeep, a post office box, and a rented storage unit in Seattle. I was constantly on the move, racking up miles and tracing a predictable pattern across the map from year to year: After Mount Baker, I would spend May and June in Alaska, then head back to the Cascades for July. In August I would be off to South America, usually Bolivia, before returning to the Cascades again in September for the tail end of the summer peak season. October, or "Rocktober" as it is known in the guiding community, was when work slowed down and we got to pursue our own climbing. For me, this usually meant a few weeks with friends on the big walls of Yosemite National Park. November and December were also slow so I would take an American Mountain Guides Association course, then pick up whatever work I could in Joshua Tree and Red Rock Canyon while waiting for ice climbing season. Once the ice was in, I worked almost nonstop from January until the middle of March, guiding clients in Ouray, Colorado, and the Sierra Nevada range in California. As the weather warmed, I'd bounce back and forth between Joshua Tree and Red Rock, before finally making the trek northwest to the Cascades to do it all over again.

It was fitting that the Cascades had become the waypoint for the different legs of my annual migration; like many alpine guides in the American northwest, I got my start there. Typically, you build your skills and experience on Mount Baker, one of the snowiest places on earth, and then you begin to expand your range. Along the way you develop a familiarity with the mountain—and in my case a fondness for it—and you always end up coming back again and again to see your old friend (preferably in the summer). Earlier in my career, no matter how miserable the conditions were, I'd think, *I can't believe they're paying me to go to Mount Baker!* and I'd happily head up to the glaciers. It was a dream come true to be guiding there—to be guiding anywhere—and for years the romance of that dream was powerful enough to overshadow the rest of the (often difficult) reality.

But this year something was different. For the first time I found myself thinking: *Do I really have to go back up there?*

Yes, I did. Guiding was still a dream come true, but I couldn't deny that the excitement of it had begun to fade and the reality was wearing on me, not so much physically as mentally and emotionally. When I first started, I didn't care that I was making less than $20,000 a year—I was doing what I loved, why worry about money?—but now the financial limitations felt stifling (at the time I was making a whopping $26,000 a year). There was the hassle of always being on the move—the cumulative psychological toll of not having a home, a place to settle in and relax, if only for a short while.

And I was lonely.

This was probably the hardest thing to admit to myself. I'm an outgoing person—I love being around people and making new connections—and I was working in a profession where my job involved being with people 24/7, often in intense and extreme conditions, for days or weeks on end. I was meeting new clients all the time and I had friends throughout the guiding community. But in the U.S., that community is decentralized because the geography is so vast, unlike in Europe where the Alps are relatively compact and there are established community hubs like Chamonix. For guides in North America, it's not uncommon to be with clients and colleagues nonstop for several weeks, then suddenly find yourself completely alone until your next trip, as I was that day in Red Rock Canyon.

It wasn't the first time I'd felt lonely, and it wasn't the first time I'd thought about the constraints guiding put on the relationships in my life, but it was the first time I seriously contemplated what those constraints meant for my future. For one thing, I missed my family. They lived in Michigan, where I grew up, and I only saw them once or twice a year. I wanted to be closer to them and to spend more time with them. I wanted to start a family of my own someday. But how could I meet a nice Jewish girl and sustain a long-term relationship when I was spending more and more time each year leading expeditions in Alaska, Bolivia and Ecuador? I had to admit that my prospects weren't looking good in this regard. If I was serious about finding a wife and having kids, what did this mean for my guiding career? It was a question I'd put off for years, because I suspected I wouldn't like the answer.

To be clear, I'm not suggesting that American mountain guides can't have both long careers and fulfilling family lives, because they can and do—and in fact, many of my colleagues have done just that. But striking the crucial balance is difficult, even under the best circumstances. I'd always understood this on an intellectual level. The more difficult step was coming to terms with it on an emotional level so that I could be completely honest with myself about what I ultimately wanted to get out of life and whether those goals were compatible with guiding.

In retrospect, the desert rainstorm was the perfect backdrop for this soul-searching. Not because the rain was a novel event—in my years as a guide, I was rained on and snowed on in the deserts of the American Southwest more than you would believe possible—but because it was a natural interlude, an opportunity to take a break from my routine and think about other things. That's what the tourists missed when they fled back to the city. For them the rain was unexpected and unpleasant, and they escaped as quickly as they could to the security of a more familiar environment. But I understood the storm was a natural part of the desert climate. I knew the conditions could change at any moment, and I was prepared for when they inevitably did. Because I was prepared, I was content to wait for the rain to pass, even if it meant enduring a little cold in the meantime. This combination of preparedness and long-term perspective had been crucial to my success as a guide, and it helped me realize I had some important decisions to make before I moved on to the Cascades.

My first decision was easy: I needed a new tent. One that didn't leak.

With the rain showing no signs of letting up and the wind gusting harder and harder, water dripped steadily through worn-out seam sealant, until my sleeping bag and I were thoroughly soaked. I finally sought shelter in my Jeep. As I sat there with the engine running and the heater blasting the chill out of my body, I grappled with a more important—and more difficult—question: was it time to stop guiding and find a new career?

At first, I couldn't believe I was even considering this. I'd been hooked on climbing since I was 11 years old, when my family took a vacation to the Keweenaw Peninsula in northern Michigan. Early in the trip I discovered a boulder field nearby to where we were staying. I spent many hours scrambling up and down the giant sandstone blocks, and would have been perfectly happy doing nothing else for the entire vacation. After that, I devoured every climbing magazine, book, and video I could get my hands on. I learned the important knots and practiced tying them over and over, while wishing I lived somewhere less topographically deprived than Michigan's lower peninsula. With no mountains to explore, I incessantly badgered my parents to drive me to the indoor climbing gym.

When I turned 14, I bought a pair of ice climbing boots and crampons from a magazine, and waited impatiently for them to arrive. When they did, I strapped the spikes to my new boots and practiced my French mountaineering technique by climbing up a sand dune on the shore of Lake Michigan, an hour from my parents' summer home, happily oblivious to the funny looks I got from the summertime tourists. The following winter I got to take those boots and crampons ice climbing with a guide for four days in North Conway, New Hampshire. I idolized the guide and the lifestyle, and I was absolutely enchanted by the beauty of the White Mountains. When I eventually became a guide myself years later, the accomplishment was even more rewarding than I had imagined it would be. I was climbing all the time, traveling the world, meeting people and doing amazing things—*and that was my job*. I wanted it to be my career forever.

Truth be told, I had suspected while teaching my first mountaineering course that I might not have it in me to be a guide for a lifetime, because the course clearly presented the full and uncompromising reality of what I was getting into. Mount Baker was miserable in the springtime, yes, but we all understood that a blizzard on Denali would be worse. Every trip into the mountains was an uncertain proposition. Depending on the season, we would risk avalanches, rock fall, altitude sickness, lightning strikes, hidden crevasses. Glaciers were alive, always shifting and changing, always treacherous.

Guiding was hard work, and it was dangerous. We would be responsible not only for our own safety in a hazardous environment, but for the safety of our clients and everyone in our party. It was, quite literally, a matter of life and death.

I accepted all of this, because that's what it meant to be a successful guide—accepting the hardships and the risks and doing what I could to minimize them, while recognizing that I could never completely eliminate them. It was a profound realization about the importance of balancing risk and reward, and it made me love guiding even more. It also made me aware of the internal tension I would feel throughout my career as a guide—the tension between the powerful romance of this thing I loved so much and the difficult reality of it. I went into the profession with my eyes wide open, confident I could take the challenges in stride, and for years I did.

In my Jeep, still damp and exhausted, I went back and forth between romance and reality until I could no longer deny what I felt: it was time for a change.

It is tempting to point to the discomfort of that particular day as the catalyst for my decision, but really there was no singular reason, no sudden moment of clarity. It was the culmination of everything I've described—the physical stress, the ever-present risks, the migratory lifestyle, the pay, the loneliness—and even with all these things foremost in my mind, I resisted the conclusion I had just come to. I wasn't really going to give up my dream job ... was I?

I drove to the West Charleston Library in Las Vegas to contemplate what I might do after guiding. If I went through with this decision to pursue a different direction in life, it would be a radical change. I was more than three years removed from the traditional professional world. Prior to guiding, my post-college work experience was a hodgepodge: internships in broadcast journalism and public relations; a brief contract position cyber-casting Mount Everest expeditions for a mountaineering website; and nine months at an investment bank in San Francisco, which I left when the guide service offered me a job. I hadn't followed a typical career path, and I knew my résumé wasn't going to open many doors on its own. I would need a plan to ensure a successful transition.

Graduate school was the first thing that came to mind. I remembered something my dad, had told me years earlier when I applied to college: "An undergraduate degree is education for life," he said. "Graduate school is education for a profession." If this was my opportunity to prepare for a new profession, then I didn't want a degree with a narrow focus; I wanted something versatile, something that would offer me the broadest range of possibilities. It was the same philosophy I tried to convey to my clients about what to carry on an alpine climb. An air mattress was comfortable to put between the snow and your sleeping bag, but a foam pad weighed less, was almost as comfortable, and could double as a splint for a broken bone in an emergency. Versatility was the key to this calculus. It made the simple foam pad the better piece of gear, and it helped me decide that an MBA was my best choice for graduate school. With an MBA I saw opportunities to work in marketing, the non-profit world, sales, or even finance. I didn't know what my next career would be, but I felt confident I would have plenty of options to explore.

By the time the rain cleared up late in the day, I was ready to move on. I'd made my decision to give up guiding. It would take time, patience, and careful planning to make the transition. I would research MBA programs and submit my applications in the fall. If accepted, I'd be back in school a year after that. In the meantime I would continue guiding, and I would continue to appreciate everything I loved about the work and the lifestyle.

The next three years unfolded almost exactly as planned, a rare occurrence indeed. At first, I followed my normal migratory path. I guided in the Cascades, Alaska, and South America, setting aside time here and there between trips to prepare my graduate school applications. Only when the acceptance letters arrived did I start to look forward to life after guiding. My last expeditions before grad school were in Alaska, with a quick trip to Australia. When I returned, I cleared out my storage unit in Seattle and drove cross-country to American University in Washington, D.C., where I earned my MBA from the Kogod School of Business.

∧

As I wrote at the beginning of this introduction, it was never my intention to go into business with my dad. It seems strange to say this now, given how much I've learned from working with him and how much I've enjoyed the experience, but I arrived at American University thoroughly seduced by the success of the businessmen I'd had as clients when I was guiding. They tended to be entrepreneurs, executives, investment bankers, and the like, and I was pretty sure I'd follow a similar path to success by working at a bank or a start-up (maybe my own). It wasn't until I took a course on family businesses a few semesters into my MBA that I seriously considered becoming a financial advisor and joining my dad.

I'd always known my dad was successful, and I knew he built his success by helping his clients achieve their long-term financial goals, first as a stock broker and then as a financial advisor, but growing up I never really understood what he did on a day-to-day basis (confidentiality requirements meant that he couldn't share many details of his work). The more we talked seriously about the possibility of me joining the business and the more I learned about what it entailed, the more I came to understand the significance of his accomplishments. By helping his clients increase their wealth, he had become wealthy himself. At Roney & Company, the Detroit-based brokerage firm where he started his career, he produced more revenue over a 22-year period than anyone else in the company. After Raymond James acquired Roney & Company, he was consistently in the top three of more than a thousand financial advisors. *Crain's Detroit Business* recognized him as one of the top financial advisors in Michigan, and he made *Barron's* national "Top 1000 Advisors" list two years in a row.

Yes, my dad's success was alluring to me, and yes, I wanted to achieve a similar measure of success for myself, but in the end my decision to join his practice was based on something much more profound. Ultimately, I realized that the true foundation of his success is a combination of integrity, optimism and his belief that if you take a long-term view and do what is fundamentally correct on an ongoing basis, then your probability of success increases over time. This is more than an investment philosophy or a business philosophy—it's a philosophy of life, which I share.

Growing up, I had experienced the power of my dad's philosophy firsthand. The way he treated his employees, clients and business associates was the way he treated my mom, my sister and me, and the way he treated everyone he met: with respect, encouragement and love. All of his accomplishments, personal and professional, are rooted in this philosophy. I realized that working alongside him would be an opportunity to build my new career on that same foundation.

My dad, Paul, began his career 46 years ago. Since then, the economy and the stock markets have risen and fallen and risen again, unpredictable in the short term but broadly cyclical in the long term. During my nine years with Hack Wealth Management of Raymond James, we've experienced the worst financial crisis since the Great Depression, a severe recession and a lackluster recovery, while at the same time the stock markets have gone to extreme lows and highs. Through it all my dad's philosophy hasn't changed, and it continues to produce significant success for those who adhere to it.

Of course, there are no guarantees in investing. Maybe the past 46 years were unique and going forward things will change. Or maybe not. As one of my dad's investor role models, Sir John Templeton, said, "The four most dangerous words in investing are: 'this time it's different.' "

Paul and I don't believe the fundamentals of investing will be different in the future. We believe individuals can continue to achieve their financial goals by adhering to the same principles of taking a long-term view and consistently doing what is fundamentally correct—the principles that have produced so much success for our clients up to now.

Which brings me to the reason I'm writing this book: I believe our philosophy is what sets us apart as a wealth management firm, and I believe it's worth talking about. I want people to understand how we think about investing. If you already subscribe to our philosophy, I want to reinforce it and reaffirm your confidence that it's the right approach to securing your future. If you don't subscribe to it, I want to educate you in the hope that you too can be successful in achieving your financial goals.

In the following chapters I will explain the concepts behind our philosophy and illustrate them with examples of what we believe people have done right and wrong in different circumstances. (While these stories are based on real people, I've changed the names and some details to protect their privacy.) Each chapter is organized around a phase of the stock market cycle—the peak before a decline, the declining (bear) market, the market bottom, the growth (bull) market and the new market peak. We've found that each phase tends to present particular challenges to the long-term investor, even as the specific details of every market cycle are unique. By highlighting these common challenges and presenting examples of associated successes and failures, I will demonstrate how our philosophy has helped our clients avoid making inappropriate decisions at critical times. When in doubt, take a moment to revisit the stories I've shared in these pages and be reassured that, while difficult times are inevitable, we believe our commitment to consistently doing what is fundamentally correct really does make a difference in the long run.

While preparing to write this book, I asked my dad to describe what we do, not in technical terms or business jargon, but in the simplest way he could. He thought for a moment and said: "We're guiding people on a journey to manage wealth."

This idea, the wealth management journey, struck me as

the perfect metaphor—not just because long-term investing *is* a journey, one that takes time and follows a path with many ups and downs, but also because it acknowledges the importance of having a trusted and experienced guide. As financial advisors, our mission is to help you succeed on your journey to manage wealth, just as it was my mission as a mountain guide to help my clients return safely from each and every expedition.

I had never considered the connection between my two careers before that moment, but now the link seems obvious: in many ways, being a mountain guide prepared me to become a financial advisor. It's not a stretch to say that I lived the principles of my dad's philosophy every day in the mountains, that I internalized it and made it my own. Conditions could change at any moment, and it was my job to advise my clients on the best course of action in the face of these inevitable challenges. To do this, I relied on the fundamentals of guiding to ensure our safety, and I always took the long-term view when assessing risk. With so many parallels between mountain climbing and our "journey to manage wealth," I've included a few of my guiding experiences to help further illustrate the core concepts of our philosophy where appropriate.

This isn't a how-to guide to the minutia of investing or a prescriptive checklist for success. Rather, it's the story of what makes us unique in our business—and what makes our relationship with each other, and with our clients, so special.

For me, the story began in a rainstorm in the Nevada desert; for my dad, it began 46 years ago when he took a leap of faith and joined a brokerage firm straight out of college. Together, we're united in our commitment to our clients and by our shared belief that taking a long-term view and doing what is fundamentally correct is the best way to increase the chances of achieving realistic financial goals on the journey to manage wealth—and in life. This is as much the story of those who stayed true to our philosophy and succeeded, as it is those who didn't see the journey through and failed.

1

THE LONG-TERM INVESTOR

n 1946, my dad was diagnosed with polio, which caused partial paralysis of his left leg. He was 15 months old. Over the next 20 years, he would undergo 14 surgeries to help him regain some strength and mobility in his leg. While most of us grow up getting stronger and more agile with each passing year, he endured setback after setback. I've often tried to imagine what it was like for him to have a disease steal his childhood from him, and every time I think about it, my imagination fails me. Whatever hardships I've had in life pale in comparison.

My dad and I have talked about his experience with polio many times throughout the years. We spoke about it again when I interviewed him for this book. "It was my first lesson in the importance of long-term thinking," he said. "Growing up, it seemed like I was always in a cast or wearing a leg brace, but my parents never allowed me to use those things as an excuse for being inactive. They didn't want any disability that I had to hold me back as a child—or maybe in some respects more importantly, as an adult. They had the foresight to understand what I needed to do to make my leg stronger. They understood it would take a long time, that sometimes it would be painful or uncomfortable for me, and that I would be better off in the long run.

"So I went to school, I participated in physical education and sports with the rest of my classmates. I remember multiple occasions riding my bicycle through the neighborhood with a cast on—much to my doctor's dismay, I'm sure. I never considered myself limited, and I led a normal, active childhood, which carried over into an active adulthood. There were certain activities I couldn't do, like skiing and ice skating, things that required better balance, but I never considered those issues important. I even became a very good pilot.

"I was fortunate that my parents took a long-term view of my recovery. It had a tremendous impact on how I learned to view the world. I saw that I could participate as fully as anyone else, if I was persistent enough, and I saw that what I did today affected my ability to participate in the future. I learned that if I wanted to succeed at something, I had to consistently apply myself to doing the things that would give me the best chance of achieving my goal. The more consistent I was and the more I thought about future consequences, the more success I had. Over time it just became natural to apply this perspective to everything."

When I was growing up, my dad would take me on long bike tours that he organized. We would ride 25, 30, or even 50 miles. I was always excited to be invited along on these rides with him and his friends. They were adults and athletes, and as a boy I felt like I was in a big-league sporting event. Sometimes I had to pedal as hard as I could to keep up with them, especially when we were riding uphill. I didn't realize until much later that my dad was working hard on these rides, too, because most of his power was coming from just one leg. Looking back, I don't know how he made riding 50 miles and climbing all those hills look so effortless. I learned a lot about perseverance on those rides without really being aware of it at the time. They were formative experiences, because my dad was teaching me through his example of perseverance what was possible in life. This became the foundation for how I would train for the endurance required to climb mountains later in life.

It's no exaggeration to say that my dad takes a long-term view on everything. When he went to college, he knew he wanted to be a stockbroker. He also knew trading stocks was a difficult profession to succeed in, so he earned a degree in accounting "as a fallback," he said. "I was thinking ahead. I always had a numbers orientation, and figured I could get a 'real' job as an accountant in the all-too-likely event that I failed as a broker. I didn't know I wouldn't even be able to get an entry-level job as a stockbroker because I didn't have any sales experience, I wasn't married, I didn't have children. After graduation, when no one would hire me to be a broker, I thought, 'Well, at least I'm prepared to do something else. At least I can be a CPA.' "

It never came to that, however, because in the end Paul got hired as a back-office worker at Roney & Company, which led to an analyst position in the research department.

"It turned out that my accounting background was very valuable in the research department," he told me. "I would look at the numbers for all these public companies, and then I would travel around to meet with their executives. You can go through numbers, but there is no substitute for meeting with people. If you think about your life, when you have good things happening and you're excited about it, you talk about it. And when things aren't going well, for whatever reason, you sort of avoid those subjects. So if you have all the statistical information and meet with people, you can get a sense of whether things are good or things are not good. It was great experience, and it really helped me to understand the importance of not just a strong balance sheet, but good management.

"The other thing I did in the research department, I would analyze client portfolios and advise clients on stocks and asset allocations. This was how I got registered to be a broker, because I needed a Series 7 license in order to talk to clients. Coming from the research side and with my ingrained long-term orientation, I developed a very fundamental approach to investing—conservative, long-term growth rather than going for short-term aggressive growth, which exposed a portfolio to more volatility and greater risk. The clients I advised tended to do well in their investments, and I actually started to build a clientele while I was still in the research department. After a couple years, I was making more money as a broker than as a research analyst, so I made the transition to being a broker full-time. It was an unusual start, and a difficult start. It's always a difficult start."

The rest, as they say, is history. It wasn't the path my dad had imagined, but by taking a long-term view from the outset he was prepared to make the most of the opportunities that presented themselves along the way. In time he was able to achieve his goal of becoming a stockbroker, despite what seemed like an insurmountable setback at the beginning.

Around 1980, he started doing seminars on financial planning as a new way to help clients manage their investments. He pioneered this area at Roney & Company, and the response was tremendous. These seminars brought in many new clients over time, making financial planning services a larger and larger part of it his business.

A major turning point came in the early 1990s when Paul

began working with professional money managers. He had recently taken on the pension account for a publicly traded company, and he felt there was a fiduciary responsibility inherent to managing a pension plan that required a different level of management than his individual client accounts.

"There was nothing wrong with what we were doing for our individual clients," he explained. "Those accounts were doing very well, and we were providing great service, but I just felt the pension needed a dedicated manager."

A brief explanation of the difference between mutual funds and money managers is probably in order here. Money managers and mutual fund portfolio managers are often the same person. The difference between a mutual fund and a separately managed account lies in the nature of the ownership of the underlying securities. With a mutual fund, you own a share of the fund and so participate collectively with all the other owners in the gains and losses of the stocks that the fund owns; you don't own any of the fund's stocks. With a money manager, you are more likely to have a more concentrated portfolio, 40-100 stocks on average, that you own directly. This direct ownership is the advantage of the managed account. Since you own the individual stocks, the money manager can buy and sell these stocks—or purchase new stocks for the portfolio—on your behalf at any time. The key is that the strategy of the managed money account is tailored to your individual investment goals.

"So I hired a money manager out of Chicago to manage the pension portfolio," Paul said. "We would analyze the portfolio and set the strategy, and the money manager would execute our strategy. This was our first managed-money account, and it worked very well.

"Actually, that's an understatement," he said. "I looked at the money manager's performance over time and I compared it to my performance with individual stocks and the performance of the mutual funds I bought for a lot of my clients, and I found that the money manager consistently did better, sometimes significantly better. And I realized that made sense. The money manager had people who only managed money, that's all they did. I, on the other hand, had several different responsibilities: I prospected for new clients, I serviced existing clients, and I managed money. All these responsibilities meant that I couldn't just focus on stocks. That's why I was putting a lot of clients into mutual funds, because I'd understood for a long time that it made sense to hire other people to manage money. So I came to the conclusion that the best long-term solution was to use money managers for my clients who had enough assets to qualify for it, and I began to transition those clients from individual stocks and mutual funds to money managers, which back then was new territory for individual investors. Institutional investors had been doing it for a long time, and today it's how most financial advisors manage money, but when I started doing it, it certainly wasn't prevalent for individuals.

"Switching to money managers did several things for my business," Paul continued. "First, the results were typically better than other results, so my clients stayed with me. Our retention rates were already pretty high at that point, but they went up even more. Second, our results attracted a lot of new clients—at one point our business was growing 40% a year—and we found that we could successfully work with many more clients than before, because money managers were managing the money and we were able to focus our attention on guiding people through the journey. In the long run, this proved to be the biggest turning point in my career."

Using money managers has become the standard for financial advisors across the industry, but the practice itself doesn't guarantee success. Ultimately, the money manager is just one part of the investment strategy and asset allocation plan developed by the client's financial advisor. If the strategy and asset allocation plan are not fundamentally sound, then even the best money manager will be hard-pressed to achieve satisfactory results. The methods may have changed over time, but the basic principles of investing and the nature of the stock market are the same as they ever were. There are no shortcuts to success on the wealth management journey. That's why our long-term approach continues to be so important, and so effective.

^

During his 46 years in the investment business, my dad has held many professional titles—research analyst, stock broker, financial advisor, wealth manager, senior vice president—but perhaps the best way to describe his career is to call him what he's always been: a long-term investor.

What does it mean to be a long-term investor? For us, it means we believe the stock market moves in cycles of growth and contraction, one following the other as surely as spring follows winter. A market cycle typically averages three to five years, and broad trends of growth or contraction can last even longer. History has shown that over the course of time (one or more market cycles), the market tends to rise more than it falls.

The short-term movements of the market are completely unpredictable, which makes it impossible to reliably time the market by investing only during periods of growth and getting out of stocks during declines. You can't tell which direction the market is headed from one day to the next.

With this in mind, we believe the best approach to investing is to ignore short-term movements of the market and focus instead on the market's long-term trend of growth. If the market rises more than it falls, then the longer you stay invested, the greater your chances of taking advantage of that steady climb.

Being a long-term investor means recognizing that successful investing is a journey that takes time to complete, a journey with no shortcuts. It means having clearly defined financial objectives for your journey and an investment plan designed around those objectives. It means staying committed to the journey even when your emotional response to the short-term price fluctuations you're supposed to ignore tempts you to try to time the market.

My dad started his own journey by studying the great investors of the modern age—Sir John Templeton and Peter Lynch, and later Warren Buffett. He learned the fundamentals of investing by following in their footsteps, just as I've learned by following in his. These fundamentals have led us to practice a style of wealth management we refer to in jest as "fairly boring":

We favor stocks and use bonds, other fixed income vehicles and alternative investments to mitigate volatility in order to get a balance between risk and reward that is appropriate for each client's objectives and personal risk tolerance.

We are proponents of investing in good, well-managed companies, based on the theory that earnings drive stock prices; and we don't advocate investing in things we don't understand.

We believe it's important to have a well-diversified portfolio consisting of different styles of investments, with the goal of lowering the overall volatility of the total portfolio.

We believe in having clearly defined financial objectives and a plan for achieving them.

And we believe the best path to success for most investors is to become as fully invested in the stock market as your objectives and risk tolerance allow and to stay that way for as long as possible.

This journey may sound boring to some people. But boring or not, it has been successful for our clients for over four and a half decades, and we're confident it will continue to be successful going forward.

⌃

The long-term investor's wealth management journey begins with a simple assessment: If your investment time horizon is at least three to five years, we recommend committing to the long-term investment approach until your objectives change. On the other hand, if your time horizon is shorter than three to five years, it is probably more appropriate to structure (or restructure) your portfolio according to your short-term goals. Since most of us fall into the former category, the long-term approach makes sense in most cases.

Our argument in favor of this position is based on the two assumptions about the nature of the market I introduced earlier: (1) over the long term (defined as one or more market cycles), stock prices tend to rise more than they fall;

and (2) the short-term movements of the market are impossible to predict.

The assumption that stocks tend to rise more than they fall is well founded in historical precedent. If you look at a chart of the market spanning the past 100+ years, there is a clear and dramatic upward trajectory—a steady climb. There have been many peaks and valleys along the way, and future growth isn't guaranteed, but in the absence of a radical departure from the past it seems reasonable to assume the long-term trend of the steady climb will continue.

At the same time, experience has shown the market doesn't rise or fall in an orderly fashion, a fact that is readily apparent when you focus on the fluctuations within a market cycle. These fluctuations can be extreme from day to day and week to week, and are not generally a function of the intrinsic values of publicly traded companies changing on a daily basis. Instead, short-term price changes are caused more by changes in investor perceptions, which can be influenced by any number of factors ranging from economic indicators and political events to the weather. (In early 2014, for example, a prolonged, severe and unusually cold winter across much of the country is believed to have contributed to a contraction in the U.S. economy and a corresponding decline in the stock market. Then, in the months that followed, the Dow climbed to record highs yet again, eclipsing 18,000 before year's end.) With so many variables in play, there is simply no way to predict how or when these factors will cause the market to rise or fall, or by how much. As my father often says, "In the short term, the market will do what we least expect—so expect the unexpected, and you won't be disappointed."

So how do we resolve the tension between our two assumptions—between the steady climb we've observed over the long term and the market's persistent unpredictability in the short term?

The answer, as you may have guessed, is time. We can't anticipate what the market will do from day to day, and we've seen that stock prices tend to rise over the course of one or more market cycles. If we accept these two premises, then the logical way to overcome short-term unpredictability and realize the long-term gains of the steady climb is to be invested in the market for as much time as possible. Time doesn't reduce our exposure to short-term volatility, but rather increases the probability that our investments will grow by outlasting whatever volatility we encounter along the way. Yes, it's possible for the value of a portfolio to decline over a market cycle, but we've consistently observed that the longer money is invested, the greater the probability the economy, and subsequently the stock market, will do well. That's why, if you have the luxury of time on your side, our philosophy is to consistently make fundamentally sound investments and always take the long-term view.

We realize this is easier said than done. Human nature

is biased toward short-term thinking, and our decisions are more often influenced by emotion than reason.

For example, we all have a natural tendency to look back on the events of the recent past and assume they will continue into the future. It's a feedback loop: our conviction that the future will be more like the past increases the longer the past has been consistent. When things are going well, we feel good and assume they will continue to go well. When things are not going so well, we become unhappy and often lose sight of the fact that all things change in time. This innate psychological bias affects spending patterns, voting attitudes and investing decisions. It can also lead us to make inappropriate decisions at the least opportune time—like abandoning investments in fundamentally sound companies to chase "hot" stocks during a bubble, or getting out of a declining market just before the next rally. Everyone is vulnerable to this kind of thinking, regardless of intellect or sophistication. It's a difficult bias to overcome.

I've experienced it firsthand, both in my career as a financial advisor and while working as a mountain guide. In the mountains, it's easy to focus so intently on your immediate situation and short-term desires that you lose sight of what's most important in the long run—namely, returning safely from each and every expedition. If you're only thinking about reaching the summit of the current climb, you can be tempted to take inappropriate risks and make poor decisions that could jeopardize your life, and the lives of everyone in your party. The danger of succumbing to short-term biases is never more apparent than when you're 2,000 feet up a climb and the weather starts to deteriorate. Intellectually you know the wise decision is to retreat, but emotionally you've invested so much in the climb you want to push on. The only way to quiet those emotions is to think long term. The history of successful (and still living) mountain climbers is full of examples of turning back within sight of the summit in order to survive.

The common practice of trying to time the market is a prominent example of the short-term bias we see in investing. Many individual investors and money managers aim to be invested in stocks only during periods of growth, and to be out of the market during periods of decline. In principle this sounds great, and I admit the appeal is undeniable: if we possessed a high degree of accuracy in predicting the short-term movements of the market, it stands to reason we could accumulate wealth at a much faster rate. In practice, however, we've seen that people who attempt to time the market generally achieve lower overall rates of return than those who stay fully invested over the long term. Still, market timing remains a great temptation, and it's a topic we address with our clients on a regular basis. Even Paul admits to having attempted it on a few occasions early in his career, though he ultimately concluded that it was an exercise in futility.

∧

When he first started as a financial advisor, Paul was fortunate to have some clients who had accumulated significant wealth before they hired him. These clients were well-versed in the fundamental principles of investing that would become the long-term journey we practice today. One of these clients, Maxwell, helped Paul learn the importance of not trying to time the market.

One day, Paul suggested selling a stock in Maxwell's portfolio. The stock, Tandy Corporation (which is now Radio Shack), had done well for a long time, but Paul's most recent analysis of the company led him to believe that the stock was now overvalued and would most likely underperform in the future. Maxwell agreed. "Okay," he said, "we'll sell the stock. What are we going to buy to replace it?"

"I don't have anything in mind right now," Paul admitted. "I thought we'd just go to cash and wait until we found something better."

"Don't sell yet," Maxwell said. "When you find another stock to buy, we'll sell, but not until then. I never want to be out of the market."

Maxwell and Paul talked about this decision at length. Maxwell explained that he was confident he would make more money in the long run by staying fully invested in the market. He was adamantly opposed to timing the market, even if the timing was the result of just not being able to find a stock to buy.

This left a lasting impression on my dad, and he still talks about it today as a formative moment in his career. Maxwell was absolutely convinced of the wisdom of his strategy, he was fully committed to it and *he was right*—in the long run *he did* make more money by staying fully invested than if he'd gone to cash, even temporarily.

Maxwell, who became one of my dad's closest friends, also helped to reinforce other principles learned from the great investors, such as the importance of a diversified portfolio and the importance of appropriately balancing risk and reward based on long-term objectives. In fact, diversification was the reason he hired my father in the first place. Maxwell had made an investment in a privately held company that went on to do exceptionally well. When the private firm was later acquired by a publicly traded company, Maxwell received publicly traded stock in exchange for his investment. At the time, this stock made up 80% of his net worth, which he decided was too large a position for him to have in any one investment. Maxwell preferred to have a diversified portfolio of stocks, typically 10 to 12 stocks, and he didn't want any one of them to account for more than 10% of the value of his portfolio. So Maxwell called upon Paul to help him sell off this new stock and reinvest the money in other stocks to rebalance his portfolio, which subsequently outperformed most of the market indices over the next 30 years.

In the process of rebalancing Maxwell's portfolio, Maxwell and Paul had occasion to discuss the question of risk tolerance. Paul had found a promising company with a lot of potential for growth in its stock price. The downside, of course, was a greater amount of risk. There is a direct relationship between risk and reward in investing: the more reward an investor receives, the greater the attendant risks of the investment. Paul understood this principle well, and he thought Maxwell would agree that the stock's potential for high rewards were worth the risk. But Maxwell said no to the stock, much to Paul's surprise.

"It's a good investment," Maxwell said, "just not for me at this point in my life. It would be great for someone looking to create wealth and take the risks associated with doing that. There's no need for me to take those kinds of risks anymore." Maxwell had already accumulated wealth. His objective was to manage his wealth effectively to provide long-term security for himself and his family, and his tolerance for risk in his investments had changed accordingly.

Another of Paul's very successful clients, Richard, made the same point under different circumstances. Richard had accumulated a significant amount of wealth through real estate and business ventures, the equivalent of more than $11 million today: he enjoyed a very comfortable lifestyle, as you might imagine. He first came to Paul for an analysis of a business he was considering buying. After a thorough review, Paul recommended to Richard that he buy the business. Richard bought the business, then hired Paul to be his financial advisor.

As it turned out, Richard wasn't relying only on my dad's opinion to make the decision on his prospective acquisition— he had also sought opinions from three other people, all much more experienced than Paul. (My dad was just 26 years old at the time, and had only recently made the transition to being a full-time financial advisor.) Paul's analysis was consistent with the other three, and this earned him a great deal of respect from Richard.

When he ultimately became a client, Richard told Paul that he preferred a conservative investment approach. "I don't need to double my money," Richard said. "There's no point. If I double it, nothing really changes in my lifetime. I've got two homes, I belong to a country club, I travel a lot. I'm not going to buy another house or join another country club, and I can't travel any more than I already do.

"But what happens if I lose half my money?" he asked. "Then my financial security is diminished and I can't do the things I'm doing now. That's a big risk to take when I don't really have anything to gain except more money."

Richard saw no upside to doubling his wealth, but he understood there was a lot of downside to losing half of it. This perspective had led him to reconsider his risk tolerance as part of his overall wealth management plan. It's a principle we continue to use to advise our clients today.

∧

It's important to note that all investment strategies entail some form of risk. These risks are easy to understand at the extremes of the spectrum. At the sew-the-money-in-the-mattress extreme, the money earns nothing and loses its value if there's any inflation at all. At the other extreme are highly speculative investments. Most strategies fall somewhere in between, each representing varying degrees of risk and reward.

As financial advisors, our job is to help our clients chose the strategies that give them the highest probability of achieving success on their wealth management journey without taking on more risk than they're comfortable with. In order to do this, we must have a clear understanding of each client's objectives and level of tolerance for risk. This understanding is key to putting together the right asset allocation plan.

Once a client's initial asset allocation plan has been implemented, the journey has begun. It's never an easy journey, given the unpredictability of the market. The clients who stay committed to it for the long term understand the nature of investing. They understand our principles and our process. They understand their portfolio is not an end in itself, but rather a means to an end. The wealth management journey is not about making money for the sake of making money; it's about making money to achieve the financial goals our clients have set to secure their future.

Unfortunately, the short-term biases inherent to human nature can cause even the most committed investor to lose sight of his or her long-term objectives. The movements of the stock market are exciting and they evoke strong emotional reactions that can divert our attention and distract us from our goals. By approaching the investment process as a journey along a path with many ups and downs, a journey we know will take time to complete, we are better prepared to guide our clients through the inevitable challenges they will face along the way—and our clients are better prepared to take those challenges in stride and stay the course.

I'm reminded of the time I was hired by an engineer from Tacoma, Washington to guide the Ptarmigan Traverse, a 35-mile route through the high country of the North Cascades from Glacier Peak to Cascade Pass. The route travels over glaciers, high saddles and heather slopes. It requires technical climbing and lots of bushwhacking, because mostly there's no established trail to follow. It took us six days to complete the traverse, and it rained and snowed every day. For most of the trip, visibility was 30 feet or less. I spent the entire time glued to my map and compass, charting our course through the wilderness with a combination of patience and determination. It was a huge accomplishment for me, and a reminder of the importance of relying on sound fundamentals when the going gets tough.

The road to success is never a smooth one. No market ever moves in a straight line. The path to the summit of a mountain is never as easy or safe as it appears from the ground. How do we give ourselves the best chance to succeed? By consistently adhering to the fundamental principles of our discipline, whether it be mountain climbing or investing, and by remembering to always take the long-term view.

⌃

CHAPTER 1
Summary Points

▸ Managing wealth through long-term investing is a journey. It takes time and follows a path with many ups and downs.

▸ The stock market moves in cycles of growth and contraction. These cycles typically average three to five years, but they can be shorter or much longer.

▸ In the long term, the stock market tends to rise more than it falls—a steady climb.

▸ In the short term, the movements of the market are unpredictable: stock prices don't rise or fall in an orderly fashion. You can never tell which way the market is headed tomorrow.

- Human nature is biased toward short-term thinking and influenced more by emotion than by reason.

- We all have a cognitive bias that causes us to assume the events of the recent past will continue into the future. The longer the past has been consistent, the stronger our conviction that the future will be the same. This bias temps us to be less cautious when things are going well, and to be overly conservative when they aren't.

- Don't try to time the market. Ignore short-term movements and focus instead on the market's long-term trend of growth. The longer you stay invested in the market, the greater your chances of taking advantage of the steady climb.

- There are no shortcuts to success on the wealth management journey. Invest for the long term in a diversified portfolio that appropriately balances risk and reward.

- There is more downside to losing half your wealth than there is to doubling it.

THE BEAR MARKET

As long-term investors we accept the fact that the stock market moves in cycles, typically lasting three to five years. We also accept the fact that we can't predict when a cycle will begin or end, or what specific path the market will follow along the way. What we do know is that market cycles progress through a common series of phases: there is the peak before a decline, called a market top or market high, which is both the end of one cycle and the beginning of the next; the declining market, often referred to as a bear market; the bottom of the decline; the growth market, often referred to as a bull market; and, finally, the new peak. It's important to be aware of these phases, because each one tends to present challenges that can make it difficult to stay committed to the principles of our wealth management journey.

Sometimes it's easy to tell which phase the market is in, especially if we can see a clear upward or downward trend in the recent past. The longer the market has been growing or declining, the more obvious the trend seems (and the more likely we are to incorrectly assume it will continue indefinitely into the future, an innate psychological bias you will recall from Chapter 1). At other times, when the market is highly volatile, it can be harder to see which way the trend is headed until after the fact. Market highs and market bottoms are a different matter altogether. By definition, these are singular events—the highest and lowest points of a trend. They are impossible to predict, and they can be identified only in retrospect.

This chapter focuses on the challenges long-term investors face during bear markets. These times are never fun for our clients or for us—after all, no one likes to see their net worth decline by any amount—but they are as much an integral part of the wealth management journey as the bull markets. One key to success on this journey is in how we respond to setbacks along the way. Do we abandon our long-term approach because of short-term anxiety? Or do we reaffirm our commitment to that approach, confident that consistently doing what is fundamentally right will give us the best chance of achieving our goals? It's not always easy to choose the latter option, but experience has shown it to be more effective than other alternatives—and not only with respect to investing in the stock market.

^

As a mountain guide, my clients and I often faced adversity that threatened the success of our expeditions. Sometimes these situations were simple to overcome, like minor equipment malfunctions or brief squalls of unexpected bad weather. At other times they were literally matters of life and death. In every case, it was my commitment to conservative and fundamentally sound guiding and climbing practices, and to taking the long-term view, that ensured our safety. We didn't reach the summit every time, but in climbing the summit is only a short-term goal; the long-term goal is always to come back alive.

I faced a particularly difficult challenge on my seventh Alaskan expedition, a climb up the West Buttress of Denali, the highest summit in North America. Our party consisted of me and two other guides and nine clients. It was mid June when we arrived at base camp on the southeast fork of Kahiltna Glacier by bush plane. After unloading the plane, we buried 10 days' worth of extra food in the snow and marked it with wands so we could find it when we returned to the camp at the end of our climb three weeks later.

Situated at 7,200 feet elevation, base camp on Denali is

an amazingly diverse community, where climbers from all over the world gather in preparation for setting off into the Alaska Range. During the summer season, it's not uncommon to encounter skilled alpinists eyeing first ascents, ambitious parties attempting to earn a place on the Seven Summits list by summiting each of the highest peaks on each of the seven continents, professional guides and their clients, and even casual tourists making day trips by ski plane to marvel at the bustling encampment high on the glacier. The climbing parties build their snow walls close together, and there is a strong sense of camaraderie and competition.

Climbing Denali is a serious undertaking. The West Buttress is the easiest and most popular route to the summit, but it is by no means easy. The route is 16.5 miles one way and gains over 13,000 feet of elevation, traversing glaciers, steep snow fields, and exposed ridges in a harsh sub-polar climate where conditions can change at any moment and without warning. Bad weather is one of the biggest hazards, and the primary reason that, on average, only about 50% of the more than 1,000 people attempting the West Buttress annually are successful. To account for weather delays and ensure our clients the greatest chance of reaching the summit, we were equipped for up to three weeks on the mountain, plus the extra food we'd cached at base camp. Each of us would be shouldering at least a 60-pound backpack and pulling a small sled loaded with more gear; together, each sled-and-backpack combination weighed upwards of 120 pounds.

Moving that much weight up the mountain requires ascending in a series of stages called "carries." Each carry goes something like this: One day you load up some of your gear, set out from camp, and climb several hours to where you want to establish your next camp. You cache the gear you've carried with you in the snow and then descend back to your old camp to sleep. The next day, weather permitting, you break camp, pack up the rest of your gear, and climb up to your cache site, where you build snow walls and set up your new camp. Then you take a rest day to recover and prepare for the next carry. It's a methodical and reliable way to move heavy loads up a big mountain, and it helps with acclimatization too.

On this expedition we hiked in four-person teams, one guide with three clients roped together for safety. Our first carry was uneventful as we shuttled gear and ourselves from base camp to a camp at 8,000 feet. After a rest day we made the climb to 11,000 feet and cached gear there, then returned to our camp to sleep.

The next day we got a weather report over the radio that a storm was coming, so we quickly broke camp and started the seven-hour climb to our cache at 11,000 feet, intending to have our new camp dug in before the storm arrived. In our haste we made a major mistake: instead of packing each rope team to be self-sufficient, we failed to distribute the gear evenly, something I wouldn't discover until several hours later.

We made steady progress up the mountain in decent weather for about an hour, with my rope team trailing the others. Then, suddenly, we were in one of the worst snowstorms I had ever experienced. We continued in tight formation as the storm intensified. I had to stop when the bailing on one of my client's crampons broke. I self-belayed back to him and was able to repair the crampon, but during the 15-minute delay the other two rope teams moved far ahead and visibility had reduced to almost nothing.

Concerned, but not worried, I pulled out my compass and began following the bearings I had plotted the day before. This worked well until the compass iced up. I wiped it clean with my glove, but it iced up again almost immediately, and I knew we couldn't go any farther in the storm. The snow was coming down too fast, the winds were too strong and the chances of making a grave mistake were too high. I called the team to a halt and told them we would make camp where we were and hunker down for what I hoped would just be the night.

As we unpacked the sleds and set up camp, I realized the mistake we'd made earlier in not properly distributing the gear among the rope teams. We had only one three-person tent for the four of us. We could all squeeze in, but it would be tight quarters.

And, more critically, we had no fuel for our stove.

Now I was worried. With only eight quart-size water bottles between the four us and no fuel to melt snow for drinking water, the threat of dehydration was a serious danger. We needed an alternative way to turn snow into drinking water. I realized that if we only drank half the water in our bottles, then refilled them with snow and shook them well and kept the bottles between our legs inside our sleeping bags, our body heat would be enough to melt the slushy mixture. I drilled these instructions into my clients. The process was uncomfortable and laborious—the bottles were cold lumps between our legs, and the task of leaving the cramped confines of the tent to collect snow in the middle of a high-altitude blizzard was even less enjoyable than it sounds—but I was glad to have thought of a solution. In addition to keeping us hydrated, the process took on the feeling of a regimen, which helped to pass the time while the storm raged. This became more important the longer the storm went on. We didn't have much else to do, other than shift body positions occasionally and take turns going out into the blizzard every few hours to dig out the tent as the snow piled up on it faster than I had ever imagined possible.

Storms in the Alaska Range are unpredictable terrors. Born of strong winds blowing inland from the Aleutian Islands and surges of polar air sweeping down from the Arctic Circle, they're often quick to develop and slow to dissipate. They can last for days, and sometimes a week or more. As we huddled in the tent over night and well into the next day, the storm only grew stronger. The wind roared like a jet engine. The snow walls we'd built around our camp bore the brunt of it, but still the tent flapped and shuddered around us. There was nothing to do but keep to our hydration regimen and take turns digging. The more snow we shoveled off the tent, the more fell from the sky. It seemed the storm would go on forever.

On the third day, one of the clients went out to dig and accidentally slashed a hole in the tent fabric with the shovel. Snow and frigid air burst into the tent. I sealed the hole with duct tape and wedged my body against the breach. Outwardly I remained calm, but in my head I was furious—not at the client but at myself. This was my responsibility. A simple mistake, a deviation from the fundamentals of guiding, had put us in this situation. I couldn't go back and undo that mistake, so I tried to focus on the positives: We were alive. We were warm. We had shelter and plenty of food and a system for melting snow into drinking water that was proving even more effective than I'd hoped. I was confident we could outlast the storm, but that confidence wasn't enough to make me feel better.

That night I kept my back pressed against the damaged tent wall. I remember the weight of the snow outside pressing back, the chill of my water bottle slowly thawing in my sleeping bag, the others cramped and close in the tiny space of our nylon cocoon. I was exhausted but I couldn't sleep. I've never felt so alone as I did that night. I stayed awake thinking about my mistake and hoping for the storm to pass. And the next morning it did.

At dawn the wind quieted, the skies cleared. We emerged from the tent and found one of the other rope teams camped less than 50 yards away. They'd been there the whole time, invisible in the blinding snow and impossible to hear over the howling wind. My clients and I talked about what to do and made the decision to climb up and rejoin the other rope teams that morning. It was a joyous reunion. We made camp at 11,000 feet and took a rest day to recover from the storm. Then we pushed on up the mountain. Eventually, all but one person in our party would reach the summit on that trip.

After 19 days on the mountain we returned safely to base camp to find that our expedition wasn't quite over: we couldn't fly out because smoke from forest fires in Siberia had blown across the Bering Sea and visibility on the glacier was too poor for the bush pilots to land. The smoke didn't clear for five days, and we were glad to have the extra food we'd cached at the beginning of the trip. Only after we took off from the glacier did I finally relax. We had faced adversity and made it through. I would lead many more expeditions in the course of my guiding career, but none would be as difficult, stressful, frightening and ultimately rewarding as that one.

I came away from the experience with a renewed commitment to certain fundamentals inherent to both climbing and guiding. It would have been easy to blame the storm for the difficulties we faced, but I understood the storm wasn't the problem. It was a natural element of the mountain environment and nothing more. We knew we would encounter storms during the expedition—there are always storms on Denali—and we had planned accordingly. The problem arose when we failed to properly execute on our plan. Simple as it was, our mistake left us vulnerable to the unpredictability of the weather. If the weather had held until we reached our cache at 11,000 feet and made camp, we probably never would have noticed what we'd done wrong. But when the storm hit, we were exposed, and we faced a more serious situation than if we'd taken care to divide the gear correctly among the rope teams in the first place. It was a powerful reminder of the importance of always doing what is fundamentally correct. So much is unpredictable in the mountains—the weather, the conditions of the rock and ice and snow, how clients respond to altitude, exertion and exposure—that a single poor decision at the wrong time jeopardized the success of our expedition.

The same concept applies to being a long-term investor during a bear market. Bear markets are like the storm I faced on Denali—unpredictable and unpleasant, but not unexpected. The fundamentals of investing don't change during a downturn any more than the fundamentals of climbing and guiding change during a snowstorm. If we understand those fundamentals and are committed to them, and if we have clear objectives and a long-term plan for achieving our objectives, then we are well equipped and well prepared to overcome the challenges of a bear market, which are a natural part of the wealth management journey. We must trust the fundamentals that have brought us this far on the journey, and, as long as our objectives haven't changed, we must stick to the plan we've formulated to achieve those objectives over the long term, even if it is emotionally difficult to do so in the short term.

It's natural to feel anxious when the market is declining, just as it's natural to feel happy when the market is rising. These feelings are part of our natural human tendency to project the recent past into the future. When the market is rising, we're happy with the situation because we assume it will continue, even though as long-term investors we've accepted the fact that the market is cyclical and we know a downturn is inevitable. Our intellectual understanding of the nature of the market is all too easily overshadowed by the psychological and emotional factors that bias us toward short-term thinking. When the market is rising, it's rising *now* and we feel good about it *now* and we assume tomorrow will be the same, and we're pleased to discover that tomorrow *is* the same, for the most part, day after day for as long as the trend persists— until one day it isn't the same. Then suddenly, we realize that we've passed the market high but no one told us, no one even knew it was the high, and now the market is falling and we don't feel good about it and we're convinced tomorrow will be the same forever, just as we were when the market was rising. Now instead of being happy we're afraid, because we perceive the bear market to be a threat to our financial security. It's a terrible feeling, and one of the main reasons people lose sight of their long-term objectives during a downturn. We look for ways to mitigate the threat we're facing as quickly as possible, without regard for the consequences our actions could have down the road. Fear makes us shortsighted.

In down markets, Paul and I often hear from clients who find themselves questioning their risk tolerance and their asset allocation plans. The more severe and prolonged the market decline, the more clients we hear from, and they're all wondering the same thing: Is it time to get out of stocks?

Our response is to ask if the client's financial objectives have changed, or if the time frame for achieving those objectives has changed. If the answer is no—and it almost always is—then we believe there is no reason to change the client's asset allocation plan to reduce their exposure to stocks. Remember, consistency is an important part of the wealth management journey—consistently adhering to the fundamentals of sound investing, consistently executing on a long-term investment plan, consistently being invested in the stock market for the long term. Arbitrarily changing one's financial objectives and asset allocation plan because of a significant rise or fall in stocks is just another form of timing the market, a practice we strongly oppose.

The most dramatic downturn I've experienced since becoming a financial advisor occurred between October 2007 and March 2009, the worst decline since the Great Depression. When the market started to deteriorate, I had only been in the business for about a year; by 2009, when the panic and hysteria finally ended, I had to constantly remind myself that extreme, 3-standard-deviation events weren't a normal occurrence in the market cycle, my experience notwithstanding. During that time it wasn't unusual for clients to arrive at our offices unannounced, typically in a panic and having not slept well the night before. They came to us fully convinced that the only solution to their discomfort was to eliminate all the stocks in their portfolio. We understood their anxiety, but we also believed that getting out of the market in the midst of the downturn would likely hurt their chances of achieving their long-term objectives more than it would help. (Peter Lynch, the well-known investor and one-time manager of the Fidelity Magellan Fund, has said, "People who exit the stock market to avoid a decline are odds on favorites to miss the next rally." Numerous studies—and our own experience— have shown time and again that he was right.) We were confident that the economy would eventually recover and the stock market would rebound, but of course we couldn't guarantee these things or predict when they would happen. The only thing we knew for sure was that people who sold their stocks would be locking in their losses, something they would likely regret after the market turned around. It was up to us to guide them through the difficult conditions they were facing, to calm their fears and keep them from selling their stocks at fire-sale prices.

It was a challenging year and a half. We counseled our clients just as we would have during any other bear market: we went back to the fundamentals of their financial objectives and we reviewed how their asset allocation plans were structured to achieve those objectives—a diversified approach, sound investments in good, well-managed companies. We reminded them that the market is cyclical in the long term and unpredictable in the short term. We reminded them that, historically, the market rises more than it falls over the course of many cycles, the downturn of the moment notwithstanding, and we reminded them that the patient long-term investor has historically been rewarded.

In the end, the clients that trusted us and adhered to the principles of the wealth management journey *were* rewarded. The economy stabilized and stock prices began a steady climb that eventually returned them to record levels, where they remain as of the writing of this book. Those who stayed appropriately invested for the duration, difficult as it was, are likely wealthier now than they were before the downturn.

⌃

As successful as our approach has been over the years, we sometimes have clients tell us they're thinking about changing financial advisors. This doesn't happen often—an estimated

97% of our clients stay with us on an annual basis—but it does happen on occasion, and we've found that it happens most often during down markets, when anxiety levels are high and people are naturally more inclined to make decisions based solely on emotion rather than reason.

This isn't to suggest that people never have good reasons for making a change. Sometimes they do. The best reason to change financial advisors is when the relationship is a bad fit in terms of objectives, risk tolerance, investment philosophy or even personality. There's a saying: "Show me your friends and I'll tell you who you are." It's a fact of life that people tend to gravitate to others who are like them, because they can relate to them. We've found this to be true in our industry, as it is in most relationship-based businesses. That's why we've made it part of our practice to begin every potential client relationship with an extensive interview process. Through this process the prospective client is interviewing us as much as we are interviewing him or her. The goal is to ensure that both sides are comfortable with the relationship from the outset. The people who gravitate to us tend to be individuals and families who understand the principles of long-term investing and share our belief that there are no real shortcuts to success on the wealth management journey. As a result, we've formed long and lasting relationships—friendships even—with many of our clients and their families over the years. A good fit is so important. If it isn't there to begin with, it's hard to develop the level of trust necessary to sustain an effective partnership through the challenges that inevitably are part of the journey, especially when the market is in decline. In such cases it's usually best for the client to make a change.

When a client approaches us in the middle of a down market and says he or she is thinking about changing financial advisors, we do our best to understand why. Most of the time it's not about the fit between our philosophy and the client's objectives; instead, it is simply another side effect of the anxiety the client naturally feels in response to his or her portfolio losing value as the market falls. It's a more drastic response than the urge to alter one's asset allocation plan, but not fundamentally different—and certainly not more likely to produce a favorable outcome in the long run. Yes, there are other firms and other advisors who do what we do, and many of them also do it well. And yes, it's tempting to think someone else might reveal a solution to what troubles us, especially if there is an aura of prestige associated with that person or firm. It's the promise of better circumstances on the road not taken, the feeling that the grass is greener on the other side of the fence. Yet in reality there are limits to what can be accomplished within in any given phase of the market, because the fundamentals of investing are the same for everyone. Sometimes the client understands this and decides to stay, assured once more that we are the best partners to guide them on their wealth management journey. Occasionally, the client decides he or she just needs to make a change. While we're sorry to see these clients go, we respect their decision and appreciate that they were willing to come to us and have the difficult conversation about it. It's a much bigger disappointment when clients leave without ever having that conversation with us.

∧

I consider myself fortunate to have summited Denali during my career as a mountain guide. The view from 20,237 feet is breathtaking, and not just because the atmosphere is so thin at that altitude. The peaks of the Alaska Range unfurl across the landscape below you in every direction, each unique in its own way: Mount Foraker's massive hump; Mount Huntington's pyramidal geometry; the mammoth walls of the Ruth Gorge reflecting in the midnight sun as they tower over miles and miles of brilliant white glacial ice. The view never gets old.

Standing atop a coveted peak is an experience so powerful that even the most seasoned climbers can find themselves overwhelmed by the euphoria of it. In such moments it's easy to forget that you've only reached the halfway point of your journey: you still have to get down safely.

Descending from a mountain can be more dangerous than climbing it. To return from the summit we must rely on the same fundamentals that brought us there in the first place. If we deviate from those fundamentals during the inevitable descent, we put ourselves and our future climbing goals at risk, just as abandoning the principles of the wealth management journey during a bear market puts the long-term investor's financial goals at risk. There are no shortcuts back to base camp from the summit of Denali, and there are no shortcuts to success in investing.

History has taught us that the stock market moves in cycles. The cyclical nature of the stock market means every peak in prices is followed by a decline, just as every market bottom is followed by a period of growth. We'd all prefer to time the market, to enjoy only the climbs to each peak and to avoid the declines, but experience has shown this to be impossible. That's why success on the wealth management journey is measured not by how high we climb on a single peak, but by how we conduct ourselves throughout the course of the entire journey.

Remember, this is a journey that takes time. The longer our investment time frame, the more market cycles we will encounter—peak, decline, bottom, growth, peak, and so on. Most of us will see these phases come and go several times over, and we must be prepared to respond effectively to each one. This means adhering to the fundamental principles of long-term investing in every situation, whether we're thrilling at a bull market's ascent or anxious about a bear market's decline. No matter what the market is doing, our approach must be to do what we have always done: invest in good companies, manage asset allocation plans according to each client's long-term objectives, ignore short-term fluctuations and let time resolve the extremes. It isn't always easy emotionally, especially during the downturns, but historically it has been very effective.

∧

CHAPTER 2
Summary Points

▸ Every market cycle is unique in its specifics, but they all progress through four common phases: the peak before a decline (the market top), a period of decline (a bear market), the bottom of the decline and a period of growth (a bull market).

▸ The longer our investment time frame, the more market cycles we will encounter on the wealth management journey.

▸ Bear markets are always challenging, but they are a natural part of the wealth management journey.

- It's natural to feel anxious when the market is declining. This isn't a reason to change your investment objectives or asset allocation plan.

- The fundamentals of investing don't change during a bear market.

- No matter what the market is doing, the long-term investor's approach remains the same: invest in good companies, manage asset allocation plans according to risk tolerance and financial objectives, ignore short-term fluctuations and let time resolve the extremes.

THE MARKET BOTTOM

On March 5, 2009, the Dow Jones Industrial Average closed at 6,594.44. Stocks had been on a downward trajectory for 18 months and counting, and in that time the Dow had lost 53% of its value, falling from a record-setting peak of 14,164 on October 9, 2007. The prevailing mood among financial pundits, investors, clients and just about the entire country was overwhelmingly negative. I'd heard a prediction a few weeks earlier that the index would drop another 2,000 points before the market bottomed out, so this particular day's close didn't get much attention beyond the usual nightly news updates, which noted with a sense of resignation that stocks had fallen yet again (cue the wah-wah trombones, as Kai Ryssdal might have said on *Marketplace*).

It was—or it seemed to be—just another all-too-familiar down day on Wall Street.

In fact, March 5th *wasn't* just another down day on Wall Street; it was actually something more significant: the market bottom, the lowest point of the decline, the last day of the bear market. When stocks resumed trading the next morning, it would be the beginning of the next bull market, a period of growth that would see the stock market regain all the ground it had lost and climb once more into record territory. Investors should have celebrated the March 5th closing bell, but no one did. Why not? Because no one knew March 5th was the market bottom until later, after the bull market was well underway.

Looking back on this experience reinforces everything I've learned from my dad about how to successfully navigate the inherent uncertainties of the wealth management journey. It's a powerful reminder that market bottoms, like market peaks, can't be predicted; they only become apparent in retrospect.

Given the unpredictability of market bottoms, you can't really have a strategy for dealing with them as separate from the bear market that precedes them, since you don't know you've hit the bottom until it's already in the past, and by then it's too late to do anything about it. Investors who get out of stocks during a decline in an attempt to time the market usually find themselves scrambling to get back in after a turnaround has already begun, having missed some of the best days of the rally in the process.

Being out of the market on the best days has a significant impact on a portfolio's overall performance: Studies have repeatedly shown that missing as few as 10 of the best days of a 10-year period can reduce an investor's rate of return by a significant margin. How significant? Between 1994 and 2013, for example, missing the 10 best days would have lowered an investor's rate of return for the period from 9.2% to 5.5%. Missing the 20 best days would have lowered that return even further, to just 3%. Worse, missing 40 or more of the best days would have resulted in a negative rate of return.

This is why Maxwell told my dad 40 years ago, "I never want to be out of the market," because he understood that missing even a few good days would hurt his chances of success in the long run. This is why Paul and I say, "it's time, not timing, that rewards the long-term investor," and why we believe it's imperative to take an investment approach that enables our clients to ride through market bottoms so that they are able to fully participate in the gains of the growth markets that follow.

Over the years, many of our clients have adhered to the principles of the wealth management journey with respect to the market bottoms they've encountered along the way. One client in particular, Philip, epitomizes these clients; he has a particularly keen understanding of the nature of long-term investing. Paul and I met with Philip in the midst of the

2007–2009 decline. Although he wasn't thrilled by the losses he was seeing on his quarterly statements, neither was he inclined to change his investment strategy. (Philip had been a client for many years at this point. He'd been very successful, both in his investing and in his business, and his approach to life was very much in line with our philosophy—do what's right, and you'll get the right results.) During our meeting he brought up the market's mounting losses, not to complain about what the market was doing but to tell us he understood why it was important to stay invested. He accepted the fact that declines—even declines as severe as the one we were experiencing—were part of the investing process, and that no one could predict when the bottom would happen.

"The market's not what I'm investing in," he told us. "I'm investing in companies, and I think we've made good investments. The economy's going to turn around. When it does, these companies will do more business, they'll be more profitable, and I'm confident the value of my ownership stake will grow to reflect these things." He was paraphrasing exactly the fundamentally sound, long-term investing mindset I've set out to articulate in this book. Success wasn't guaranteed, but he believed this approach—our approach—would see his investments safely through the downturn and the bottom and position him to make the most of the next growth period. He was right.

Not everyone has the same intuitive grasp of these

concepts as Philip; in fact, most people don't. This is perfectly understandable. As I've mentioned, human beings have several natural psychological biases working against long-term thinking. It takes time to learn the concepts of the wealth management journey and put them into practice, and it's easy to fall back into short-term thinking in the midst of a crisis (which is, of course, the most inopportune time to do so). That's what makes a guide so important, someone who understands the philosophical and technical concepts as well as the emotional challenges of dealing with uncertainty; someone who is prepared to help you through the most difficult parts of the journey, no matter what the circumstances.

∧

As Paul and I counseled our clients through the darkest days of 2008 and early 2009, I found myself thinking back to a defining moment of my mountain guiding career, when the U.S. Navy tried to lower me out of a helicopter onto an icy volcano. This was in late summer of 2001. I had just completed two back-to-back guiding trips on Mount Baker, a 10,781-foot glaciated volcanic peak in the North Cascade Mountains in Washington. I was sitting at home in Bellingham, when I got an urgent call from the operations manager of my guide service. One of my fellow guides was up on the mountain and had just witnessed a four-person rope team on the north side of the peak fall into a crevasse at 8,600 feet. The climbers were on the Coleman-Deming route, a notorious and heavily crevassed passage. The guide had used his cell phone to report the accident to our company's headquarters, which put in motion a rescue of the four climbers in the crevasse. Our service was the first to respond and would be working side by side with the U.S. Navy, local sheriff's department and Whatcom County Mountain Rescue.

"How quickly can you be geared up?" the operations manager asked me. "We need you on a helicopter as soon as possible."

The plan was for me and two other guides to meet in a field at the base of Mount Baker, where we would be picked up by a Navy helicopter and flown up the mountain to attempt a short-haul rescue. Basically, the helicopter would lower us onto the glacier near the crevasse with litters, first-aid supplies, ice climbing gear and other equipment. Our job was to stabilize the injured climbers and get them secured on the litters, and the Navy airmen would lift them up to the helicopter with a winch and evacuate them down the mountain, a standard quick-response rescue in the North Cascades.

However, there was one major complication: The weather service had reported a storm front heading toward the range, with severe winds forecast on Mount Baker. Our window to execute the short-haul rescue was closing.

Within hours, the other guides and I were aboard the helicopter, which had flown in from the Naval Air Station on nearby Whidbey Island. I remember being astonished by how loud it was inside the helicopter, so loud that the sound vibrated my chest and made my head throb. The cargo area appeared to have been stripped bare of everything but the winch, presumably to save weight.

We flew into the mountains at high speed and quickly reached the glacier just below where the four climbers were stranded. Already the winds had picked up, making for a rough approach. The crew chief gave me a hasty instructional on helicopter safety en route.

"Do *not* walk uphill after you detach from the winch!" he shouted, his words punctuated by the heavy pulse of the main rotor overhead. *"Do not walk uphill!* Do you understand?"

I nodded, picturing the huge blades slicing my body to pieces. The helicopter would be hovering level, the glacier angling up the mountainside below it. We would be lowered on the downhill side. Do not walk uphill. The crew chief was still talking. He had several more safety points for me, but I was fixated on this first one and forgot the others immediately.

The crew chief attached my harness to a carabiner at the end of the winch cable. Then he clipped in one of the other guides, my friend Andy. We would be the first to be lowered. The pilot brought us in close to the mountain, fighting to hold the aircraft steady in the gusting winds. We were only 20 or

30 feet above the glacier, but the winds were so strong they pushed the helicopter violently from side to side. Each time the crew chief started to lower us, the pilot would abort and Andy and I would be reeled back in while the pilot circled around for another attempt. We tried again and again without success, until finally we had to fly back to Whidbey Island, 30 miles away, to refuel.

By the time we returned to Mount Baker, the winds were even stronger. The crew chief tried to lower us a few more times, but it just wasn't going to happen. Instead, we dropped as much rescue gear as we could down to the climbers, who by now had managed to get out of the crevasse by walking up a steep snow ramp. Then we flew down to a lower elevation, where the pilot was able to land safely on the glacier. Andy and I and the other guide jumped out with our climbing gear and the remaining rescue equipment and the helicopter lifted off, leaving us to climb a few thousand feet back up the mountain to the victims.

When we arrived at the rescue site, one of the four climbers had already died, most likely due to a closed-head injury. The other three, two men and a woman, had suffered broken bones and other injuries and were in varying states of pain and shock. We performed basic first aid and packaged the climbers up in the litters as fast as possible, but by the time we were ready for the helicopter to return, the clouds had lowered and surrounded us, dark and ominous. The storm had arrived more quickly than expected, making an airlift impossible. We would have to spend the night on the mountain and evacuate them the next day.

We set up tents, dug snow walls to provide shelter from the wind and did our best to keep the three survivors warm, well fed and in comfortable positions, as much as was possible given their injuries—broken ankles and ribs and a broken back. The climber who'd died had been the last one on the rope team as they crossed the glacier. When he fell into the crevasse, he pulled the others in with him and they landed on top of him. He suffered a closed-head injury from the fall yet somehow he was still able to walk, and he helped the other three ascend the snow ramp out of the crevasse before succumbing to his injury. The climbers' emotions vacillated from happy that we had arrived, to angry that this had happened to them, to scared, to sad and back again. We couldn't change the nature of the situation, but we could help them get through it. We made hot tea, helped shift their sleeping bags, talked with them and cared for them throughout the night. These seemed like small things to me at the time, none of which, strictly speaking, required any technical expertise. In retrospect, I came to realize it was the care and reassurance we provided that were the most important things we did for them during that dark, cold night.

The hours passed slowly. The night was both physically and emotionally exhausting for all of us, but by morning the weather had cleared just enough that Seattle Mountain Rescue had made their way up to our position with a large team and additional rescue gear. Together we spent the entire next day bringing the climbers down the mountain to ambulances waiting at the trailhead. We used everything at our disposal to manage the descent, from the latest equipment and techniques to the simplest methods, whatever was most appropriate to the obstacle or terrain, and we got them down safely. From a technical perspective, the rescue team performed flawlessly and efficiently. And just as important as the technical aspects of the rescue, we continued to tend to the injured climbers' basic needs all through the day— keeping them dry and warm, keeping them as comfortable as possible, keeping their spirits up. We were carrying them off the mountain emotionally as well as physically.

Why did all this come to mind seven years later, when the financial markets were crumbling and the news media were yelling about the sky falling and making increasingly frightening proclamations every day?

Because, as on Mount Baker, we had come to the point where technical expertise alone would no longer suffice. The global economy was in crisis and the stock market was crashing and there was no mystery as to why. The fundamental facts were the same for everyone. There would be no helicopter rescue, no ingenious investment vehicle Paul and I could deploy to lift our clients above the collapse. We were confident in our approach, confident there would be a bottom and a recovery, confident there would be daylight on the horizon eventually, but of course we didn't know when the turnaround would happen or how low the market would go. As on the mountain, we couldn't change the nature of the situation, but there was still plenty we could do to care for our clients—not by digging shelters and splinting broken bones, but by listening to our clients' concerns and helping to calm their fears. We did this by placing the downturn, unsettling as it was, in the context of the stock market's long history, where the broadest trend, no matter how dire the short-term decline, has always been the steady upward climb. We couldn't make promises, of course, but we could review the probabilities, and explain how history has shown that the probabilities favor those who stick with the wealth management journey for the long term.

∧

In the end, almost all of our clients stayed true to the wealth management journey throughout the difficult bear market of 2007–2009. The market's steep decline, combined with all the other elements of the global financial crisis and the recession that followed, understandably caused a lot of anxiety. Every day seemed to bring more bad news about the economy, and, thanks to the human tendency to project the recent past into the future, it was easy for people to fear the worst. Despite this, our clients trusted that the economy and the stock market would recover, and that the best way for them to realize the gains of the recovery was to stay invested in stocks for the long term.

There was one exception, and fortunately he was the only one. This client, Scott, didn't understand the fundamentals of the investment process or our philosophy of the wealth management journey, and consequently he made an inappropriate decision at a most inopportune time. Scott viewed stocks as an esoteric investment. In his mind, he wasn't buying long-term ownership stakes in good, well-managed companies, with an anticipation of returns from the underlying business; he was buying the metaphorical equivalent of poker chips, the value of which fluctuated over time based on what other people were willing to pay for them, with the assumption that he would hold onto these poker chips as long as their value kept going up, then sell them if they started to lose value. He wasn't an investor, in the traditional sense; he was a speculator.

From Scott's perspective, the bear market was a catastrophe, because he only saw the potential for loss as the value of his stocks declined, and because he didn't understand that holding them for the long term would enable him to profit from the intrinsic value of the companies themselves. No amount of reasoning or explaining our philosophy could change his thinking. All he could see was the short-term fact that he'd ridden the market down from the Dow's peak above 14,000 to somewhere in the neighborhood of 6,500, and he was convinced the decline would continue to even more un-thinkable lows (remember, some in the media were predicting the Dow would go all the way down to 4,500). He'd become convinced it was time to "cut his losses" and go to cash. He thought it would be better to get out of the market before his stocks dropped even further, and he was determined to do just that.

Scott liquidated the entirety of his equity investments within ten days of the market bottom. Then, even as it became clear that the market had turned around, he stayed out of equities, refusing to reconsider his decision. It was impossi-ble for him to accept that he'd made a mistake. He told Paul, "The upside is just a temporary correction. The downside will continue."

After that, Scott never got back into the stock market. And when I say never, I mean never: the Dow was at 6,500 when he liquidated all his stocks; as of the writing of this book it's above 17,000, and still his portfolio is all in cash.

∧

If your timeframe for investing is long enough, your wealth management journey will likely include several stock market declines and bottoms along the way. While these downturns will never be enjoyable, it helps to understand that they are, in fact, a natural part of the investing process; that, historically, they have always given way to new periods of growth; and that, despite the short-term unpredictability of the market, it is possible to deal with these unpleasant phases of the cycle in ways that position you for long-term success. To effectively deal with the low points of the journey, you must accept at the outset that they are both inevitable and unpredictable. Accepting these facts enables us to help you prepare accordingly by implementing an investment plan that doesn't have to change whenever we encounter adversity in the market—a plan capable of carrying us through not just the good times, but also the most difficult times.

Still, we're all human, and that means we all have our moments of doubt, moments when the short-term biases I've talked about sneak into our thinking and challenge our commitment to the wealth management journey. Moments when we find ourselves tempted to believe those four dangerous words Sir John Templeton warned us against: *this time it's different*. If you find yourself having one of these moments in the midst of a downturn, I encourage you to reread this chapter and the previous chapter about bear markets.

Once you truly understand the principles of the wealth management journey and are able to put them into practice, you will find yourself less and less concerned with the daily movements of the market, with its short-term ups and downs. You will be less anxious when the market is in decline, and you will realize that market bottoms are irrelevant, except as historical points of reference. (After all, the only reason to care about market bottoms—and market peaks, for that matter—is if you are trying to time the market, a practice that you, as a long-term investor, understand to be fatally flawed by its very nature.) It's a perspective that can be very liberating.

ᐱ

CHAPTER 3
Summary Points

▸ You don't know when a market bottom happens until after the fact. Market bottoms can only be identified in retrospect.

▸ Investors who get out of stocks during a decline in an attempt to time the market often find themselves scrambling to get back in after a turnaround has already begun.

▸ Missing even a few of the best days of a market rally significantly lowers an investor's overall returns.

4

THE BULL MARKET

n mountaineering, big mountains tend to bring out big ambitions and strong emotions. Mount Rainier and Mont Blanc, Everest and Denali: the bigger the climb and the more famous the peak, the more obsessed people become in the pursuit of it—human psychology intersecting with topography at the ego's hungriest apex.

Everything about a big mountain is more intense: the altitude, the exposure, the conditions. Preparing for these extremes requires increasingly greater commitments of time, effort and money, to the point where it's not uncommon for people to pay tens of thousands of dollars to attempt a major summit in a far-flung corner of a distant continent, to devote months or even years to intense physical training, and to spend several weeks, if not a month or more, on the mountain. It all adds up to a powerful gravitational pull on a climber's psyche, a force that distorts reason and makes it difficult to maintain your long-term perspective even when the risks you face clearly outweigh any potential rewards. *Throw caution to the wind*, says the mountain. *Bad weather, pain and discomfort, death—what are these things compared to the glory of the summit?*

The appropriate response to such temptations might seem self-evident—*I'll stick with the more conservative, fundamentally sound approach, thanks*—but in reality it's extremely difficult to think clearly when you're in the middle of a climb and emotions are running high. In these circumstances the desire for accomplishment and ego fulfillment can cloud the judgment of even the most reasonable person, obscuring the right decision as quickly and completely as a sudden whiteout in the high country reduces visibility to zero.

The same psychology applies to bull markets, especially when they persist over many months or years. After enduring a decline, investors naturally greet a turnaround with relief. Then, as the growth phase progresses, other emotions take over: optimism, excitement and greed. The longer and steeper and higher the market's climb, the stronger these emotions become, just like a climber's obsession with a mountain. The psychological bias that made investors fearful during the bear market now has the opposite effect, making them incautious and overly optimistic. It's thrilling to be on the ascent, to see the value of your portfolio increasing, and it's all too easy to get caught up in that euphoria and make inappropriate decisions as a result.

This happened with two of Paul's clients in the late 1990s. The overall market was in a period of strong growth at the time, with many clients seeing tremendous returns from their investments, in some cases well over 20% annually, and Internet and related information technology industry stocks were rising even faster.

It is important to note that Paul had kept his clients out of Internet stocks, despite their astonishing growth. As you'll recall, one of the principles of the investment philosophy he learned by studying Templeton, Lynch and Buffett was "buy things you understand," and he didn't understand how tech startups could justify their valuations; the stock prices just didn't make sense in terms of their fundamental financial metrics. Rather than go along with the popular rush to get into tech stocks, he looked at these investments with a critical eye from the perspective of risk versus reward.

"What I saw," he told me, "was a tremendous potential for reward, but with a very high risk of failure. Very smart people were talking about paradigm shifts and the like, and I thought maybe they were right, maybe these companies will innovate their way to future earnings that justify these prices and keep the growth going, but in the end I came back to John Templeton's warning about the dangers of thinking, 'this time it's different.' I didn't believe it was different. To me, the exposure was too great. I wasn't brilliant in this regard, although I'd like to say that I was. I just felt we could get hurt a lot more than we could benefit if it ended up being a speculative bubble. And it turned out I was right."

But that vindication only came with hindsight. In the feverish run-up to the eventual dot-com collapse, many of Paul's clients approached him to ask about tech stocks. He explained to each of them his reasons against making those investments, and mostly he was successful in reassuring them that their fundamentally sound asset allocation plans gave them the best chance of achieving their long-term financial objectives. However, the two clients I mentioned, Brett and Samantha, couldn't be convinced. Both had become obsessed with the potential returns they believed they were missing. They came into Paul's office within a month of each other, and the conversations he had with each of them were almost identical.

"You know," Brett said, "I'm really not doing as well as I could be with my portfolio."

In fact, Brett was seeing close to a 26% annual return, which, Paul pointed out, was more than double the stock market's average lifetime return.

"Right," Brett said, "but if I were into the Internet stocks, I could be making 45%. I have a friend who's doing that right now."

"That may be the case," Paul said, "but my sense is that we're in a bubble, and ultimately it's going to burst. It could go on for years, I don't know, I'm not clairvoyant. I can't tell you how long these kinds of things could last, but I can tell you that I believe it's not worth the risk."

"I disagree," Brett said. "I'm sure this is what I want to do."

"Then go ahead and do it," Paul said, "but not with me. I don't want to be the one you blame if it doesn't work out. Because that's what will happen, no matter how many forms I have you sign saying it was your idea—in the end, you'll end up blaming me, and I'm not interested in being part of that. And, frankly, I don't want to participate in something that makes no sense to me."

Both Brett and Samantha appreciated Paul's integrity; nonetheless, they were determined to invest in Internet stocks, so they transferred their accounts to other firms. They left on good terms, and Paul stayed in touch with them for a long time afterward, which is how we know they both lost close to 80% of their money when the Internet bubble burst a few months later. The losses were devastating to them, and, with very few exceptions, the money they put into Internet companies was gone forever. Of course, no investors went through that period without seeing the value of their portfolios decline at least temporarily. The tech crash triggered a downturn in the broader stock market, and it's a simple fact that you can't be in equities and not go down when the market goes down. Had Brett and Samantha adhered to the asset allocation plans they'd established with Paul, they would have been insulated from the worst of the fallout, and their portfolios would have recovered when the market eventually rebounded.

^

In July of 2002, I led an expedition to the Ruth Gorge in Alaska, a spectacular 10-mile-long, mile-wide glacial cirque carved into the lower southeast flank of Denali, where steep, intimidating granite cliffs tower thousands of feet above either side of the Ruth Glacier as it flows down through the gorge. Our party consisted of myself, another guide and six clients. We flew on a ski plane to the historic Don Sheldon hut and made our base camp under clear skies. Our list of potential climbs was long—Mount Dickey, Mount Dan-Beard, maybe even the famous Moose's Tooth—but our plans were quickly laid to waste: heavy clouds began to gather over the range as the plane left us, and within hours we found ourselves socked in by a storm that would last seven days. Equal parts rain, snow and whiteout conditions, the storm was fickle but relentless. Attempting to climb the steep and difficult cliffs of the gorge was out of the question until the storm passed, so we scouted the glacier near our camp in search of crevasses. We found a few that we could safely lower into, and we took turns climbing out of the icy fissures. Although this was a moderate-ly entertaining diversion, we mostly passed time in the cook tent, telling stories, playing games and generally laughing the days away. It was good to be in the company of people that could deal heartily with such a disappointing situation.

When the storm finally cleared, the gorge and the sur-rounding mountains lay under a thick blanket of fresh snow, the cliff faces caked with an icy frosting. One look outside my tent and I knew we wouldn't be attempting any of the climbs we'd come here to do. Every route was an avalanche waiting to happen.

I broke the news to my clients: "We've been shut down by the weather," I said. "We'll have to stay in camp. Avalanche dangers are too high."

But the clients didn't want to hear it (and neither did I, honestly; I'd become just as antsy and ambitious). "We've come this far," they said. "We can't turn back without at least making an attempt." They were convinced we could force our way up, despite the perilous conditions. Intellectually they understood that the risks far outweighed the momentary vin-dication of reaching a summit, but emotionally they wanted to believe their situation was different. (Templeton's four most dangerous words apply as much in the mountains as they do in the markets.) I reasoned with them for hours before they finally accepted that our expedition had come to an end.

This was an extreme case, where the risks were so severe

and so obvious that the only prudent decision was to back down. In less extreme circumstances there isn't always an absolute right way to deal with risk, and, provided you adhere to the fundamental principles of climbing and guiding, the calculus becomes much more personal, because everyone has a different tolerance for risk. As a guide, it was my job to assess as objectively as possible the risks we faced in a given situation and then advise my clients on our options for managing those risks in ways that were appropriate for them personally, always weighing the short-term goal of any climb against the long-term imperative that everyone comes down off the mountain safely. Sometimes we turned back, sometimes we pushed ahead. The key for me was evaluating the risks of our physical environment, while also being confident that my clients were keeping the climb in perspective. If I suspected that ambition or the allure of a famous peak was beginning to cloud their judgment, I intervened, as in the Ruth Gorge.

This is what Paul tried to do for Brett and Samantha during the Internet bubble. As their guide on the wealth management journey, he assessed the situation in terms of his experience and the principles of investing he had found to be most successful over time, and he determined that the route they wanted to take was too risky for their objectives. Paul couldn't prevent them from investing in Internet stocks in the same way I was able to prevent my clients from continuing on a climb that was too dangerous, but he could and did refuse to make the investments for them as a matter of principle. They were free to take their accounts elsewhere, and they did; it was their money and ultimately the decisions about how to invest it were theirs to make as they saw fit. Even though they both ended up going in a direction my father didn't agree with, he appreciated that they were willing to come to him and talk about it.

"I'm sure they knew I wouldn't support what they wanted to do," he told me. "I had good relationships with both of them, and they really did want my advice. They listened to my opinion, but the right thing to do is often the hardest thing to convince people to do. Both of them had lost sight of their long-term goals. All they could think about was this great return they felt they were missing. They'd become blind to the risks, which turned out to be catastrophic."

Brett and Samantha weren't the first clients to abandon the principles of the wealth management journey to pursue a riskier investment strategy, and Paul knew they wouldn't be the last. When the market is growing, and especially when one sector of the market is growing faster than others, it's all too common for people to look at their portfolios, no matter how well they're doing, and think, *I could be doing better.* Usually it's because they know someone, a friend or a relative or a friend of a friend, who claims to be getting higher returns with a different firm. Perhaps the other person really is getting higher returns, but it's not an accurate comparison if you only look at the rate of return by itself; you need to know if the investment strategy and asset allocation plans are comparable. If you're 60% stocks and 40% bonds and your friend is 100% stocks and it's a rising equity market, your friend is going to be making more money than you are, that's a given, because your asset allocations aren't even remotely comparable. (Keep in mind that in a declining equity market, this same friend is going to lose more than you are.) So it's important to investigate—"investigate before you invest," as the saying goes—to find out what's really behind the numbers and how it compares to your current strategy and allocation plan, in terms of both upside and downside.

In Brett's case, his friend's 45% return was the result of a radically different asset allocation heavily weighted toward Internet and information technology stocks, one that came with a much higher risk exposure. It wasn't really an apples-to-apples comparison. To his credit, Brett understood this, which is why he asked Paul to change his asset allocation. But oftentimes people don't know how to make an accurate comparison on their own. It's easy to be swayed by seemingly impressive numbers, even though the numbers themselves don't tell the whole story, or even most of it.

Over the years we've lost a few clients to other firms this way, and it's always disappointing. "It doesn't bother me that they left," Paul said when I asked him to reflect on these situations. "What bothers me is that they had concerns and didn't talk to us about them. They were too embarrassed.

"I understand that sometimes people feel the need to make a change," he continued. "And yes, sometimes a change is for the better—something like 95% of investors change financial advisors at least once in their lifetime—but the most appropriate thing to do when you think you want to make a change is to first talk to your current advisor about your concerns. You've got somebody you've been working with for years, typically 10 or 15 years, sometimes longer. You've got a relationship, one based on trust and open communication, at least it should be. So don't be embarrassed to tell your advisor what you're thinking. Sit down with them and say, 'I got this proposal,' and let them review it with you and do a comparison, if they question the performance. And if it really is better, if it really addresses some performance aspect you're unhappy about, then maybe it's time to make a change. But the most important thing is the communication. Clients should never be embarrassed to talk to their financial advisor."

The most important thing is the communication—I can't put it any better than that. We're confident the principles of our long-term investment strategy are necessary conditions for success, but we know they don't lead to success on their own. Open communication with our clients enables us to activate those principles that give each individual client the highest probability of achieving their objectives. There's no question in my mind—and I know Paul agrees—that our most successful clients, in terms of achieving the financial objectives, have been those with whom we've carried on an active dialogue throughout the relationship. I don't mean just talking periodically. I mean regularly having open and forthright conversations about all the aspects of the wealth management journey, from the client's objectives and risk tolerance to a complete understanding of their income and assets. The honest exchange of information on an ongoing basis is what sets these relationships apart.

On a side note, it might seem like an obvious thing for a financial advisor to know what a client's assets are, but it's surprising how many people think it's better not to share important financial information with their financial advisor. It would be like hiring an accountant to do your taxes but not giving him all the information about your income and assets and deductions; he couldn't file a complete return. Or it would be like going to a doctor and not telling him all your symptoms, which would make it difficult for him to diagnose what was ailing you. We've occasionally had clients who took this approach and didn't give us a complete picture of their assets. One client, Ronald, invested with us very successfully for 10 years before he finally told us he had other assets being held in other places, with relatively low rates of return. These other assets were significant—nearly equal to the assets he'd invested with us. When Paul asked why he hadn't mentioned these assets previously, he said, "It's not money for the long term. Low-yield investments are fine. I just want to preserve it."

Ronald's mistake was not viewing all of his assets together in their totality. By separating what he thought of as "short-term" assets from his "long-term" assets and not giving us a complete picture of his financial resources, he prevented us from creating an asset allocation plan that accurately reflected his objectives. Had he been forthright in letting us know about his other assets, we would have tailored his long-term investments differently. We could have discussed the possibility of incorporating his other assets into that plan in a way he was comfortable with, perhaps increasing the total return on his complete portfolio in the long turn. Even if he had ultimately decided to keep those assets separate, just knowing about them would have given us more options to work with. This is why open communication is so important. The more information we have, in terms of both your assets and your disposition toward investing those assets, the better we'll be able to put together an asset allocation plan that gives you the highest probability of achieving your financial objectives.

I should stress that it's not necessary to invest all your assets with one financial advisor in order to have a comprehensive strategy for your total portfolio. In our experience, it's absolutely crucial to have such a strategy, and the only way to do that is to have a comprehensive view of your total portfolio, regardless of where your assets are held. As a service to our clients, we collect from them all the information about all their other investments—other brokerage firms, bank accounts, certificates of deposit—and we put together a composite showing their overall asset allocation. This composite is the complete picture of their portfolio. We offer this service and we encourage our clients to utilize it because we feel it is important for us to be able to advise them on all their investments so that their overall portfolio is in balance and diversified according to their objectives and risk tolerance. When clients don't have a comprehensive view of their portfolio, they tend to adopt different strategies for each investment, and as a result their overall portfolio doesn't have the appropriate long-term balance.

Paul often saw this kind of confusion in 2000 and 2001, after the dot-com collapse. Several clients asked him to take over management of their 401(k) accounts, which until then they had kept separate from their investments with him.

"These were clients who had adhered to our philosophy of long-term investing in their accounts with us, and those accounts had done very well over time," Paul explained. "But in their 401(k)s with other firms they'd had terrible results. What typically happened was that they invested differently in their 401(k)s than they did with us. Our approach was the same then as it is now, and the same as it's always been—conservative, long-term and predicated on investing in good, well managed companies. Instead of applying these principles to their 401(k)s, these clients decided that Internet stocks were the best place to be. So they loaded up on Internet stocks, ignoring the fundamentals that we adhered to in their investments with us, and when the Internet bubble burst, they lost the vast majority of the assets in their 401(k)s.

"It was a tragedy. This was retirement money for these people, and when they lost it, they inhibited their ability to retire and had to postpone retirement for a number of years. Having a comprehensive view of their total portfolio might have helped them understand the risks they were taking, and it might have convinced them to apply our principles to their 401(k)s. Based on the history, we know that would have been a much better outcome."

Every once in a while we'll do a composite asset allocation for a client and they'll be on board with our approach to developing a comprehensive strategy, but they just don't understand the totality of it; even when they're looking at the composite report, they continue to view each one of their investments separately. One such client, Warren, had investments with us, a bank and another brokerage firm. The plan we developed called for an overall asset allocation that was 60% equities and 40% fixed income, perfect for giving him a high probability of fulfilling his long-term objectives without taking on more risk than he was comfortable with. In order to achieve this overall allocation, however, his investments with us would be 100% equities, because he already had substantial fixed-income holdings with his bank, and his account with the other brokerage was a balance between equities and fixed income. Together, all his investments added up to the 60/40 split he wanted.

"Sounds great," Warren said after reviewing the plan and the composite asset allocation report we'd prepared for him. "So why is my account with you 100% equities? It should be 60% equities and 40% fixed income. That's what we talked about."

"Your total portfolio is the sum of its parts," Paul explained. "It's not 100% equities; only our part is 100% equities. When you add that to your bank deposits and your other brokerage account, all your assets collectively are allocated 60% equities and 40% fixed income."

But Warren continued to focus just on our part of the portfolio. "It's all equities," he said. "It can't be all equities. It has to be 60/40."

Paul walked him through the mathematical breakdown of the composite allocation several more times. "If we make our investments 60% stocks and 40% fixed income, it will change the allocation of your overall portfolio," he said. "You'll be too heavily weighted toward fixed income, closer to 50/50. That's not appropriate for you."

Warren never could understand how the pieces fit together, and eventually he transferred his accounts to another firm.

It's a similar situation when a client focuses only on the performance of individual investments, rather than on the performance of his or her total portfolio. Sometimes an investment will underperform, be it an individual stock or a group of stocks in a particular sector of the market; this is part of the nature of the market. Clients who focus too much on individual pieces of their portfolio tend to lose perspective. Instead of evaluating the overall performance of their investments against their long-term goals, they become obsessed with an underperforming asset and think we should have performed better than the market in every category, rather than in most categories. This kind of short-term thinking is a warning flag that a client is in danger of abandoning the wealth management journey altogether. We do our best to help them see the bigger picture, but those who simply don't understand the totality of their investments often find themselves unhappy in every phase of the market cycle, even periods of growth. While these clients occasionally turn into former clients, like Warren, we know that if their next financial advisor isn't able to change their thinking, they're likely to become former clients of that financial advisor as well.

⌃

As a mountain guide, I saw firsthand how easily the emotions and ambitions associated with big climbs like Denali and Mount Rainier can alter a person's ability to appropriately balance risk and reward. The expedition to the Ruth Gorge wasn't the only time clients tried to argue their way past the point of irrational risk: on both Denali and Rainier, I had clients try to pay their way past. These experiences helped me realize that the allure of the summit is a form of greed, a lust for success that pushes people to lose sight of what's important to them in the longer term.

Paul and I have seen this in the markets, too. Some clients were so seduced by the allure of big short-term returns that they lost sight of the equally big risks that came with pursuing those returns. Like Brett and Samantha, it was often the case that their friends had told them how much they had earned or what huge percentage gains they had experienced. These comparisons, whether accurate or not, play on emotion, not reason, and they can have the same effect on investors that the big mountains have on climbers.

At the end of the day, I believe no summit or climb, no amount of wealth, no percentage return or investment should ever be the basis of a person's self-worth. Comparing your situation to others—Joey climbed this peak last week, or Brad is getting 45% when I'm only getting 25% returns—only encourages the kind of short-term, emotional thinking and risk-taking that so often lead to disastrous consequences in the mountains and the markets alike.

∧

CHAPTER 4
Summary Points

▸ The emotions associated with bull markets are optimism, excitement and greed. The longer the period of growth lasts, the stronger these emotions.

▸ Optimism, excitement and greed can tempt investors to take on more risk than is appropriate for their long-term objectives.

▸ Comparing rates of return is not an accurate way to compare the performance of two portfolios. Numbers don't tell the whole story, or even most of it.

▸ Communication is the most important thing when working with a financial advisor.

▸ Always have a comprehensive view of your assets, even if some investments are managed by different financial institutions. A comprehensive view ensures your overall portfolio is in balance and diversified according to your objectives and risk tolerance.

5 / THE MARKET PEAK

am convinced there is no feeling for a climber quite as sublime as making the first ascent of a mountain. To reach the summit of an unclimbed peak, knowing you're standing where no one has stood before, is to see the world from a totally new perspective. It's a rare experience, and unbelievably fulfilling.

First ascents are uncertain endeavors, in which nothing is guaranteed. They are journeys into uncharted territory, requiring a combination of sound fundamental skills, experience and perseverance to succeed. There are no trails to follow, no route descriptions compiled by other climbers to help you find your way. There is only the mountain and its rugged terrain, often inscrutable until you begin the climb.

You are tackling a massive three-dimensional puzzle that you must solve in real time, and its important subtleties are obscured by distance and scale. Looking up from the base, you can be sure of three things: it is always further than it looks, it is always taller than it looks and it is always harder than it looks. The rest of what you need to know to reach the summit, the important details, the mountain's true nature, you will discover along the way. To unlock the puzzle you must be able to operate effectively with imperfect information, part Marco Polo and part Indiana Jones—explorer, navigator, intrepid adventurer. In an age when pre-packaged tourism has reduced many wilderness experiences to little more than glorified sightseeing jaunts, as safe and predictable as amusement park rides, the first ascent is one of the last true adventures left on our planet.

Stock market peaks don't have the same transcendent quality as unclimbed summits in remote mountain ranges, but, like market bottoms, they *do* have the power to influence how investors behave. Not surprisingly, the source of their power is emotion, as we've seen with every other phase of the market cycle. In the case of market peaks, the emotions at work are the same as those associated with bull markets— optimism, excitement and greed—but with an interesting twist: in addition to making some investors incautious and prone to taking inappropriate risks, a combination of greed and the belief that a market peak is imminent can cause others to become overly cautious and seek to "get out ahead" by reducing their equity exposure in an attempt to time the market. Either way, these temptations are at odds with the principles of the wealth management journey, and Paul and I do our best to counsel clients against them.

Early in Paul's career there was a group of 50 large blue-chip stocks that became known as the Nifty Fifty— companies like Coca-Cola, Dow Chemical, General Electric and IBM. "These companies had demonstrated solid earnings growth over long periods of time," he explained, "and as a result, investors started to view them as fundamentally different from other stocks. People called them 'one-decision' stocks, meaning the only decision you had to make was to buy the stock and hold it, because its value would just keep going up and up." And for a while that's what happened: the prices of the Nifty Fifty were bid up to 50 and 60 times earnings, prices that helped propel the bull market of the early 1970s. Even so, Paul counseled his clients against buying into the Nifty Fifty.

"I was still new to being a stockbroker back then, but with my accounting background and conservative outlook, it just didn't make sense to me that companies could sell at those kinds of multiples," he said. "I didn't understand it, so I stayed away from those investments." (It's the same logic he would later apply to Internet and tech stocks to help his clients avoid the dot-com bubble.)

This turned out to be a wise decision. The bull market of the early 1970s was followed by a prolonged bear market that lasted from 1973 to 1982, during which the Nifty Fifty tumbled to significantly lower valuations. The money that investors had poured into these stocks to bid up their prices to 50 and 60 times earnings was gone. "And not only that—a lot of the Nifty Fifty went on to underperform the market for decades," Paul noted. "Some didn't return to proper valuations until the 1990s, and their prices never again approached the extreme multiples we saw back in the '60s and '70s. Avoiding the Nifty Fifty was one of the things that helped a lot of my first clients succeed in the long run."

What stands out about Paul's experience with the Nifty Fifty, at least to me, is how quickly investors became incautious when they began to believe they could secure high returns with little or no risk. History and experience have shown this to be impossible, and yet we continue to see people underestimating the amount of risk they're taking on in the euphoria of a rising market.

"And this phenomenon isn't unique to the stock market," Paul told me. "Over the years I've had a few clients take significant portions of their liquid assets and make investments in illiquid ventures, and as a general rule these investments failed. In every case, these were clients who were successful in their own businesses and professions—real estate developers, attorneys and doctors—and they were so good at what they did that they forgot the complexity of it, and they thought, 'I've done well in my business. Why not invest in this other business?' But because they no longer saw the complexities they'd mastered in their own businesses, they forgot that every business is complex, every business takes a long time to master, even the ones that look simple from the outside.

"And so these clients invested in restaurants, or modular housing, or other ventures they didn't really have the expertise to understand. Not that they couldn't have learned the restaurant business or the modular housing business, given enough time—these were all smart people. The problem was, they thought they could master their new business ventures quickly and with a relatively small amount of effort, but in the vast majority of cases that just doesn't happen."

One of Paul's clients, Leslie, is a dramatic example. Leslie was a commercial real estate developer who had successfully developed a couple shopping centers. The shopping centers were fully paid for and Leslie, who was in his 60s, lived very well off the income from those properties. He then got involved with a manufactured housing company. Leslie became so convinced this was the ultimate investment that he mortgaged both his commercial buildings and bought letter stock in the manufactured housing company.

"I advised Leslie against this investment because I thought it was too risky for him, considering his age and long-term objectives," Paul said. "Letter stock is restricted stock that hasn't been registered with the SEC yet, and so it can't be sold publicly. If the company's product had turned out to be a success, the upside for Leslie would have been very significant, but he was taking an equally significant risk by going into debt to buy stock he couldn't liquidate. And as it turned out, the company never brought the product to market. Leslie's entire investment was worthless, but he still had the mortgages on his properties, and as a result his income was severely reduced."

Leslie's experience was a disaster that could have been avoided. He didn't need more money—he'd already achieved success; he had the assets and income he needed to live comfortably for the rest of his life. Unfortunately, he let the allure of a potential reward blind him to the risk he would expose himself to in order to pursue it. He put himself in a position to take a hit that wouldn't otherwise have been part of his wealth management journey.

When talking about these types of investing mistakes, Paul often brings up Joe Louis, the World Heavyweight Champion boxer from 1937 to 1949: "To this day, Joe Louis is considered to be one of the greatest heavyweights of all time. He had a long and outstanding career, and there's a story about an interviewer asking him what contributed to his success. Louis replied that he'd figured out a long time ago how not to get hit quite as often."

Paul and I believe it's the same with investing: if you don't take big hits on speculative or inappropriate investments, you greatly improve your chances of achieving your financial objectives over the long run.

∧

When the market has been rising steadily for a while, Paul and I always get asked a variation of the question, "Are we getting close to a top?" We don't know, of course, because the short-term movements of the market are unpredictable; but we do understand the motivation for asking. The question usually comes from clients who keep up to date on news regarding the economy and follow the movements of the market, at least to some extent. They know the market moves in cycles, they know stocks are rising, they've heard about changes in this or that economic indicator, they've been listening to speculation about what the Federal Reserve is going to do with interest rates, and on and on. From all of this information they start to imagine reasons why the market might be about to go into decline—Are price-to-earnings ratios too high? Is the market overextended on initial public offerings?—and they start thinking like market timers: "Maybe it's a good time to sell, before prices peak and we go into decline again ..."

Even though our clients know we're opposed to market timing in principle and in practice—because it simply doesn't work as a long-term strategy—the temptation toward this kind of thinking can be very strong. We have found that it grows stronger the more closely an investor follows the movements of the market and the economy from day to day and week to week. Our advice to these clients is always the same: It doesn't matter whether the next peak is tomorrow or a year from now. The things that matter are your financial objectives and your time frame for achieving those objectives. If your objectives and time frame haven't changed, and if your objectives can be achieved within your time frame, then your investing strategy shouldn't change either. Consistency over the long term is one of the keys to success on the wealth management journey.

However, the temptation to "get out ahead" can be strong, especially if the market is in a period of significant day-to-day volatility, or if a client has experienced substantial short-term gains over and above the market's long-term average returns. Consider the example of David, who came to us with 15 years until retirement. We set up an investment plan based on his objectives, and during the first three years of his plan, there was a very strong bull market. At the three-year mark, with stocks still rising, he told us he wanted to change his asset allocation to reduce his stake in equities.

"I think the market is overvalued," he said, "and I think we're due for a correction. I'd like to insulate myself from that."

"You've got 12 years until retirement, right?" Paul asked. "And your financial objectives haven't changed?"

"Right, nothing has changed," David said. "But so far my returns have been much higher than we planned for. I'm way ahead. I should lock in these gains now."

"We don't know when the market will decline," Paul said, "and we don't know how high it will go, either. But a significant rise isn't a reason to change your asset allocation. Fluctuations are part of the journey."

David understood this on an intellectual level. In fact, the reason he'd come to us in the first place was because of our long-term approach to investing. Still, by paying close attention to the short-term movements of the market and to the opinions of some financial pundits who were predicting a reversal of the growth trend, he'd begun to adopt a short-term mindset.

"So should I just sit back and ride the market down?" he asked.

"Try to look at it a different way," Paul said. "We created a good investment plan for you, and it's well implemented. You're invested in good companies. You have 12 years before you need any of these assets to live on. Will the market go down at some point during that time? History tells us it will. But history also tells us the market tends to rise more than it falls, and the probability that the market will be higher in 12 years than it is today is very strong. Historically, the patient investor has been rewarded over the long term. But if you change your asset allocation now, you won't be as well positioned to take advantage of that growth."

David ultimately resisted the temptation to make the change, and time has since proven the wisdom of this decision: in the years that followed, his portfolio performed significantly better with its original asset allocation than it would have if he'd gone forward with his attempt to time the market by reducing his equity exposure.

Sometimes we have clients come to us feeling overwhelmed by the market's volatility. While these clients are still committed to the wealth management journey in principle, in practice they've reached a point, emotionally, where they've become convinced that they've taken on too much risk, and they feel something must be done about it. The conversation with a client in this situation is pretty much the same as the one Paul had with David. In the end, the client can't be talked out of making a change to his or her asset allocation. When this happens, we find a way to restructure the client's portfolio to reduce its volatility to a point the client can live with, while maintaining the long-term consistency we have found to be so important to success. Inevitably, this means increasing the portfolio's percentage of fixed-income assets and alternative investments and reducing the exposure to equity markets. The client's total cash flow is maintained, but with less dependence on the appreciation of stock prices. The downside is that the new portfolio tends to have a lower rate of return over the long term, because it reduces the client's ability to participate in the stock market's future growth.

∧

Years ago, in the late 1990s and early 2000s, Paul published a quarterly newsletter for his clients, appropriately titled "The Long-Term Investor." While the newsletter covered a wide variety of investing-related topics over a span of almost seven years, there was one constant throughout: each issue always began with a short essay in which my father would reiterate the principles of his investing philosophy and use them to illuminate some aspect of the then-current stock market climate, often in response to questions or concerns he was hearing from his clients at the time. In one essay from mid-2001, he discussed the danger of considering too much information when making long-term decisions, particularly investment decisions. This idea of "too much information" may seem counterintuitive, because we often assume that having more information is better than having less. In fact, there is a threshold beyond which the increasing quantity of information available to an individual in a given situation becomes less important than the quality of that information and the individual's ability to convert it into useful knowledge. Once you exceed a particular threshold, having access to more information can actually impede your decision making process, because not all the information available to you will be applicable to the decision at hand, and not all of it will be of the same quality. The risk of making decisions based on irrelevant or inaccurate information increases, as does the amount of effort required to filter out the information that doesn't matter.

In the case of investing, the public is inundated with financial information now more than ever. You can read it in the *Wall Street Journal*, the *Financial Times*, *Investor's Business Daily*, *Business Week*, or any number of other print and online publications. You can watch financial news coverage 24 hours a day on television, or stream it live over the Internet. The reach of these outlets is staggering: the cable news channel CNBC is available to more than 95 million households in the United States, which in 2014 was 82% of all U.S. households with television. And that's just one channel! The result is an always-on, always-updated flood of information, only some of which is actually important to the decisions facing long-term investors. The rest is just noise.

All that noise can be distracting, as we saw with David. Here was a client who had embraced the wealth management journey, who understood declines are an integral part of the stock market cycle, and who, when we formulated a 15-year plan for him, was fully prepared to ride through the ups and downs of several cycles along the way. Philosophically and intellectually, David was positioned to have the highest probability of success, but just three years into his journey he was nearly convinced to abandon it because his emotions were swayed by an accumulation of short-term information that was ultimately irrelevant to his long-term goals.

"It was a case of too much information," Paul said when I asked him to reflect on our experience with David. "And too much of the wrong information," he added.

"Over the past 46 years, just reading the newspaper, or watching the nightly news programs and being aware of the volatility of the stock market made it difficult enough to stay invested in the stock market," Paul said. "But now investors are exposed to more information than ever before, almost all of it focused on the short term, which makes it that much more tempting to abandon the long-term journey. And so much of what passes for news is really just entertainment—I mean the commentary and opinions on company earnings reports and which direction the market is headed, things like that. Opinions that just play on investors' fears or appeal to their inclinations to be greedy. It's all conjecture, but those are the things that have really proliferated, and those are the things people seem to be paying attention to."

Paul went on to tell me about *Wall Street Week with Louis Rukeyser*, the first television show focused on Wall Street and the stock market, which debuted nationwide on PBS television in 1972 and ran for more than 30 years:

"It was, by today's standards, a pretty mundane program," he said. "It was half an hour a week on Friday night, and that was the entirety of the program. It would start out with Rukeyser doing commentary on the week's financial news, and he'd give a summary of stock market statistics. Then Rukeyser would moderate a panel discussion with financial analysts, usually three. They'd give their opinions on the market and recommend specific stocks, and they'd answer questions submitted by viewers. And at the end of the show, Rukeyser and the panelists would interview a guest expert. A lot of the analysts and guests were well-known names, huge names even—Paul Volcker was a guest expert, and Alan Greenspan, and Malcolm Forbes. It was very engaging, and very successful. It's not a coincidence that most financial news programs today have similar segments.

"But unlike most financial news today, *Wall Street Week* had an inherent orientation toward longer-term investing," Paul continued. "Sometimes there was an appeal to emotions like fear and greed, and I didn't always agree with the opinions expressed on the show, but for the most part there was nothing that would tempt you away from the wealth management journey. It was a pretty consistent message, I remember, and for a long time it was the most-watched financial news program in the country.

"Now, with so many competing sources of information, you can find an analyst or 'expert' saying pretty much anything about the stock market at any time. I've said to clients, 'Tell me what you want to hear, and I'll find someone who is saying it on CNBC.' And most of this commentary has a short-term outlook. Because that's where the drama is. Did the market go up today? Did it go down? How much? Where is it going tomorrow? What should you do about it? All this is exciting when stocks are rising and terrifying when they're falling, and it's the drama that keeps people watching and advertisers buying commercial time.

"Which isn't to say the long-term perspective is completely absent," he added. "There are still people advocating for a fundamentally sound approach to investing. It's just hard to separate their voices from all the other noise.

"So with David, he's a smart guy, and he watches the market and the economy, and he started his journey with the appropriate long-term mindset. But once he got the idea in his head that he had something to lose in the short term, this great unexpected gain, he started only listening to the commentators that were saying the market was overvalued. It wasn't hard to find those opinions, because there were plenty of people saying that at the time. And there were plenty of people saying the market would go to unbelievable highs, too. Totally conflicting opinions, all based on differing interpretations of the same information. (Both extremes were wrong, by the way.) And it's like this all the time now: too much information, too many temptations."

These temptations aren't going away, and neither is the 24/7 stream of information about what's happening in the stock market and the economy at large; it's all part of the 21st-century landscape investors must navigate. So what's the best way to deal with all this information?

First, keep in mind that an awful lot of what appears to be information in the financial news media is really entertainment, particularly when it comes to opinions on which way the market is trending. Entertainment like this can be exciting to watch, but it adds no real value to the investing process. In the long run it just creates confusion, and it's emotionally exhausting.

Second, seek out the opinions of analysts and experts who view investing as a long-term process and take a fundamentally sound approach to that process. Our favorite is Warren Buffett, who is the personification of successful long-term investing, and a role model we continually point out to our clients.

Third, and most important, keep in mind you're on a journey that will take many years to complete, and most of the information clamoring for your attention simply is not relevant to making long-term investment decisions. Each market cycle takes three to five years to complete, and a typical long-term investment plan will span several cycles. When your time frame is that long, it doesn't matter what the market does from day to day, or even over the course of a year or two. More important is whether each market cycle brings you closer to achieving your long-term goals, and whether those goals can be achieved in the appropriate time frame. This is the heart of the wealth management journey: a steady climb. It's never as exciting as the breathless speculation that accompanies the market's day-to-day ups and downs, but in the end it's a lot more satisfying.

∧

In 2003, I guided three clients on a 24-day trip into the St. Elias Mountains in Alaska with the sole purpose of finding unclimbed peaks in the range and attempting to make first ascents of them.

The St. Elias Mountains and the neighboring Wrangell Mountains to the northwest are notorious for continuously severe snowy weather and extreme remoteness. These conditions have kept much of the region untouched and undocumented. Additionally, the peaks of the St. Elias range are tall but not "Himalayan tall," so they don't attract the usual cast of Seven Summit seekers, glory hounds, and others chasing immediate gratification. This was fine by me: I'd take remote, lower and untouched over crowded, high and obvious any day. Also, the added challenges of the range meant that guided trips there tended to draw a more unique clientele, typically more experienced and more flexible.

On this particular trip I would be guiding two U.S. Air Force pilots and a medical doctor. All three arrived in extraordinary physical condition—"terminally fit" was how some of my fellow guides and I jokingly described clients who were in better shape than us—but before we could head off in search of unclimbed peaks in one of the most rugged and remote parts of the North American continent, I had to assess their climbing abilities.

We began with a day of ice climbing on the extraordinary Matanuska glacier in Alaska. As my clients swung their axes and kicked their crampons into the dry glacial ice, I was pleased to discover that all three were very competent climbers, which meant we would be able to attempt more difficult ascents.

That night, we camped next to the glacier on a dirty moraine. It was mid-June, and the mosquitos descended on us in dense, humming clouds that deserve a story unto themselves. They fed on us until we escaped the next morning and caught a ski plane from an airstrip outside of Chitna, on the edge of the Wrangell-St. Elias National Park and Preserve. We flew 100 miles over snow-capped peaks, forested slopes and rolling foothills thick with sub-alpine heather to an unnamed glacial cirque just east of the confluence of two prominent glacial tongues in the St. Elias range. We unloaded our gear and watched as the plane lifted off and disappeared over the mountains to the west.

For me, this is the moment when an expedition truly begins, the moment when you step into the unknown. The feeling is part excitement, part trepidation as the sound of the plane's engine fades into the overwhelming silence of the wilderness and a palpable sense of isolation settles over you. We had two-way radios and a satellite phone, but we were hundreds of miles from the nearest outposts of human civilization, and even farther from the nearest hospital. In the case of an emergency, there was no guarantee we'd be able to call in rescue, and no guarantee a plane would be able to reach us if the weather was bad. We were completely on our own.

Because it was the middle of June and we had full daylight almost 20 hours a day, we decided to switch to a night climbing schedule to take advantage of what little freezing would happen in the brief twilight. It was a weird sensation to watch the sun dip behind the mountains to the northwest shortly before midnight only to reappear on the northeastern horizon four hours later.

The first climb we attempted in the St. Elias range was a peak that had a perfect triangular shape, a striking lookalike for the mountain in the Paramount Pictures logo. We left camp roped together at 40-foot intervals. The wide spacing between us on the rope provided an added measure of safety, to reduce the chances that more than one member of the team would be above a crevasse at any given moment. Crevasses are big in Alaska and the Yukon, and the snow bridges over them are deceptive. It was entirely possible that one of us would punch through last winter's seasonal snow pack to find ourselves with nothing but 100 feet of dark, icy air below. If that happened, the other members of the team would throw their bodies into the snow on top of their ice axes to arrest the victim's fall. Traveling over glaciers like this is the essence of teamwork: a stronger climber might be faster than his teammates, but if he falls into a crevasse, it is the other climbers who ultimately come to his rescue.

Fortunately, the snow bridges we crossed that day were strong enough to support our weight and we didn't encounter any problems on the glacier as we hiked for almost three hours over a flat, semi frozen compression zone to the base of the mountain. The face we intended to climb was about 1,700 feet tall and transitioned from a gradual 40-degree slope to a steep, 75-degree mixture of loose rock, powder snow and aerated ice. I was confident the climbing would be well within my clients' abilities.

We started with a running belay, all of us moving simul-taneously up the 40-degree slope. I set the occasional piece of protection in the snow in case one of us fell, though no one did. When we reached the transition to the steeper face, I set our first anchor and we began climbing on belay. I would lead one rope length, then set another anchor, and the others would follow. The climbing turned out to be fun, engaging, and occasionally attention-getting, but it wasn't too serious until we reached a point just below the summit where three ridges came together to create a rare obstacle. We hadn't been able to see the details of this feature from below, and I was dismayed to discover that a double cornice lay between us and the summit.

In the mountains, a cornice is an overhanging edge of snow that forms on the leeward side of a ridge, like a frozen wave piled up by the wind. These beautiful features are as dangerous as they are visually striking. Lacking any foundation below it, the snow crest has only a tenuous connection to the ridge it forms on, making cornices one of the most unstable elements on a mountain. Merely walking on top of one can cause it to collapse, triggering an avalanche and plunging the climber off the ridge. Corniced ridges can typically be avoided by climbing on the windward side, far below the formation's potential line of fracture. On a double-corniced ridge like the one we now faced, the fragile wave of snow crests off both sides of the ridge. This formation created a potentially deadly situation we would somehow have to surmount in order to reach the summit.

I carefully evaluated the condition of the ridge, gingerly testing it on belay with solid anchors close by. It occurred to me that we could use a huge section of rope to literally saw off most of the cornice on one side of the ridge, which would open up the face below it. We could climb down and traverse under what remained of the foreshortened cornice, then ascend back up to the ridge and tag the summit. There would still be some danger, but there was no wind and no precipitation, and my clients had been moving efficiently all day, so I knew we could traverse quickly.

The four of us discussed the risks and determined that the risk-reward calculus worked out in our favor: the chances of the worst-case scenario happening were slim, while the likelihood of achieving the best-case scenario was high. There was no objective measure we could apply, but we were confident the risks were well within our subjective tolerances, with a healthy margin for error. We decided to try for the summit.

The plan worked perfectly: We cut loose one of the cornices by looping a rope over and behind the underbelly of the beast and working the cord back and forth through the snow. The cornice fell away, disintegrating as it tumbled through space. We descended from the ridge, traversed quickly and safely across the newly exposed face below, and were on the summit in less than an hour. It was an emotional experience to be the first people on the planet to stand on this particular summit and to see the world from this particular vantage point, equal parts novel and empowering. For my clients, it was the first time they had made a first ascent.

We went on to summit every peak we attempted over the course of that trip, 12 first ascents in all, and on every one of them we had to overcome some unexpected challenge or another. In retrospect it's easy to gloss over those challenges and focus only on the outcome, but I think the challenges we faced along the way were what made our eventual success so meaningful. Maybe the challenges are always what make a climb meaningful, because the fact is, there are always challenges; nothing ever goes according to plan; the mountain always surprises us.

It's the same for investors on the wealth management journey: We know what our objectives are, we know how long we have to achieve them, and we're confident the principles of long-term investing will lead us on a steady climb to success. Still, we never know exactly what sort of volatility we're going to encounter along the way. Stocks rise and fall and rise again, trending upward over time even as they remain unpredictable in the short-term, every bull market a first ascent, every peak a fleeting moment. Don't let the excitement and uncertainty of these phases tempt you to abandon your journey partway. Remember that success isn't measured by the highest peak you climb any more than it is by the lowest low you endure; it's measured by whether or not you've achieved your objectives in the appropriate time frame. The ups and downs that happen in between don't matter. As John Templeton said: "Ignore fluctuations. Don't try to outguess the market. Buy a quality portfolio and invest for the long term." Yes, it really is that simple.

∧

CHAPTER 5
Summary Points

▸ The primary emotion associated with market peaks is greed.

▸ Some investors continue to feel the excitement and optimism associated with the bull market that precedes the peak. These investors tend to take inappropriate risks.

▸ Other investors begin to feel fearful in anticipation of the eventual downturn. These investors become overly cautious and try to time the market by reducing their equity exposure before the market reaches its peak.

▸ It's easier to succeed on the wealth management journey if you don't take big hits on speculative or inappropriate investments.

▸ Be wary of information overload when it comes to financial news and commentary. Remember: much of what passes for news coverage is really just entertainment playing to investors' fears or greed.

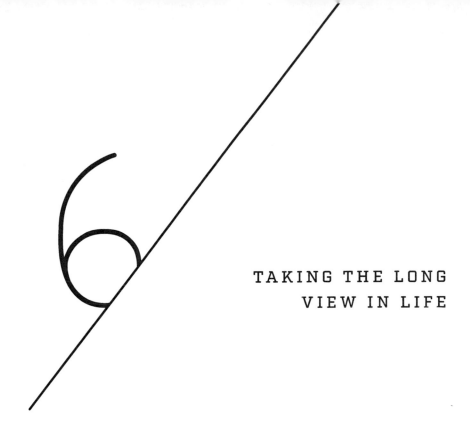

TAKING THE LONG
VIEW IN LIFE

H elping people to help themselves with dignity and respect" is the motto of Hebrew Free Loan, a Detroit non-profit organization chartered to provide interest-free loans to those in need in Michigan's Jewish community, from people needing money to fix a roof or for a medical bill all the way to assisting new immigrants wanting to start a business. Founded in 1895, the organization has a long history of success. The good will it generates is so high that the repayment rate on its loans is above 98%, and many loan recipients go on to become donors themselves. My dad served as president of the organization in the mid-1990s, and its motto could just as easily describe his own philosophy of community involvement.

During my dad's tenure as president, Hebrew Free Loan celebrated its 100th anniversary. Elie Wiesel, noted professor, author, political activist, Holocaust survivor and Nobel Peace Prize laureate, came to Detroit to speak at the celebration. I was 18 years old at the time, and I flew home from college to attend the ceremony. It was inspiring to see my dad sharing the stage with a man who had done so much to champion social justice. The connection between Elie's leadership and my dad's own commitment to helping people to help themselves was as powerful an association as any son could make.

It wasn't just my dad who demonstrated the importance of thinking about the needs of others. My mom was also a community leader, serving as president of the Shalom chapter of Detroit Hadassah and as a docent at the Detroit Institute of Arts. My parents never had to tell me or my sister to put money in a *tzedakah* (charity) box or instruct us to volunteer; they had already set a precedent by example, and we naturally followed it.

Watching my parents and their service to the community over time, I learned another one of my dad's principles: the wealth management journey doesn't have to be a selfish one. That might sound counterintuitive. After all, isn't the whole idea of the journey to make enough money so you can retire and not have to work? Yes ... and no.

Let me explain: The goal of investing is to make money, no doubt about it. For some people, this goal becomes an end in itself—the accumulation of wealth for its own sake. However, those who embrace the principles of the wealth management journey understand that making money is best viewed as a means to an end, not the end itself. They understand that the ultimate goal of the journey—and the reason most people seek to increase their wealth—is to provide financial security for themselves and their families in the long term. This broader perspective is what I mean when I say the wealth management journey doesn't have to be selfish. Often, through giving time and money and with proper financial planning, charitable work enhances the journey (and even provides a tax benefit).

Through his involvement with Hebrew Free Loan, my dad had the opportunity to interview many applicants for loans. These interviews gave him a unique insight into people's finances, their attitudes about money, the challenges they faced and their hopes. By contributing his knowledge, experience and time, he helped Hebrew Free Loan make the most of its resources, and he helped the applicants prepare to make the most of the loans they would receive. He did this not by telling them how to live their lives, but rather by helping them understand in simple terms the likely outcomes of various scenarios and what they could do to improve their chances of being successful.

"It was the same approach I took when educating my clients about the wealth management journey and the most effective habits of long-term investing," he explained. "The setting was different, and there wasn't a financial incentive for the work I was doing, but I found it very rewarding all the same. It was satisfying to be able to make a difference in people's lives by sharing the principles I'd learned in my profession—to see how that knowledge really did empower people to help themselves. It's been the same with all of my philanthropic endeavors. The time and energy I've given to the community has come back as rewards in more ways than I ever imagined possible."

When you look at the wealth management journey as more than just a quest to accumulate wealth, it changes not only the way you think about money, but also the way you think about success and the future.

My dad and I believe success can be multifaceted, if you approach it from a long-term perspective. "Making money is certainly one measure of success," my dad said, "and it's certainly gratifying, but so is making an impact on other people. That's how I've always measured my own success, beyond the financial rewards—Am I helping my clients achieve their objectives? Am I helping them to become better off in the future than they are today? To me, that's the most important thing, because that's why they came to me, to achieve financial security for their future, and if I help them to be successful in that, as many of them have been, that's my real success.

"I have clients who've been with me over 30 years," he continued, "people who are my friends. Some of them I've known since childhood, others became friends along the way. All of them trusted me, and they trusted in the journey, and they saw it through. Now they're living off the assets that we created over a long period of time. That's the essence of success, because I made a difference in their lives."

This definition of success—making a difference in the lives of others—extends beyond professional accomplishments, as I learned from my parents' service to community and philanthropic causes. Most recently I saw it play out in a very personal way, when my dad went to the hospital suffering from severe abdominal pain. The problem was a gangrenous gallbladder, but he was diagnosed incorrectly and for three days his condition worsened. We took him to another hospital, where he was diagnosed correctly and scheduled for surgery the next day. Even then, a series of frustrating interruptions occurred: he had to wait seven hours to receive an IV, and he was all but forgotten by the attending resident.

The next day the surgery was a success, with no complications. Afterward, the surgeon told my dad the infection had started to spread, and his condition would have become life-threatening in another day or two. It was an upsetting thought, and the sort of thing that might have inspired others to become angry with the medical staff who had misdiagnosed him or even pursue a lawsuit against the hospital. But my dad took a different approach: he wrote a long letter to the hospital administration, describing his experience in detail and identifying what he thought went right and what needed correction, and along with the letter he sent a generous check. His motivation wasn't to punish or penalize, it was to help the hospital improve its ability to provide quality care to all its patients in the future. He wanted to make a difference, to have a positive impact on the lives of other, and, as always, he was thinking long term.

∧

Although every wealth management journey is unique, many share in common a major milestone: retirement. This is often the milestone that determines an individual's initial financial objectives and the time frame for achieving them. In most cases, the initial objective is based on how much income the client will need to earn from investments in order to maintain his or her desired standard of living throughout retirement. It's tempting to think that the journey ends when you reach your retirement milestone, but it doesn't; it simply enters another phase. At that point, your financial objectives usually change from investing for growth to investing for income and asset preservation, and we formulate a new asset allocation plan appropriate to those objectives.

We continue to adhere to a conservative, fundamentally sound approach that allows for a healthy margin of error by underestimating future investment returns and factoring in a rate of inflation higher than the long-term historical average. A typical post-retirement asset allocation plan reduces a client's exposure to equities, but won't eliminate them entirely; in almost no cases are we comfortable with less than 30% equities in a comprehensive portfolio analysis. Based on Paul's experience over the last 46 years, we believe that a post-retirement portfolio with 30% of its assets in stocks and 70% in fixed income and alternative investments is a better long-term solution than a portfolio with no equities whatsoever. We've observed that the 30/70 portfolio tends to have no more volatility, yet it provides higher rates of return.

For most people, the assets they have when they quit working are the assets they're going to live on for the rest of their lives. Clients who understand this continue to adhere to the principles of the wealth management journey after retirement, and generally, they are well positioned to maintain or even continue to grow their assets. Unfortunately, we've had a few clients over the years who didn't understand this, and after retirement they changed their approach to managing their money. In every case the clients made inappropriate decisions that put them at risk of running out of capital in their lifetimes—this was the case whether their retirement assets were $250,000, $2.5 million, or even $10 million.

One couple in particular, Nathan and Karen, had been watching interest rates closely as they prepared to retire. They were both in their late 50s, and they had accumulated about $1 million for their retirement. This was around the year 2000, when five-year certificates of deposit (CDs) were yielding close to 6% returns. Nathan and Karen decided they wanted to take all their retirement money and put it into five-year CDs. They assumed the 6% returns would continue indefinitely, an assumption that veterans of the wealth management journey should have known better than to make. With retirement fast approaching and their financial objectives achieved, Nathan and Karen thought they were done with the journey. In their minds, all they needed to do in order to maintain their standard of living was to preserve their assets and generate an annual income of $80,000. CDs would protect their $1 million in capital, and a 6% return would yield $60,000 of income, which together with their $20,000 in combined Social Security benefits would be sufficient for them to live on for the rest of their lives without ever touching their principal.

"There's no guarantee CDs will stay at 6% indefinitely," Paul observed when Nathan and Karen asked him to change their asset allocation plan. "I can't tell you if the rates will go up, if they'll go down, or if they'll stay the same, but you have to at least consider the possibility that they'll go down. A diversified approach would be better."

Nathan and Karen insisted on putting all their money into CDs, believing that any exposure to the volatility of the stock market was too much risk for them at that point in their lives. No matter what line of reasoning he tried, Paul simply couldn't get them to see the alternative risk to which they were exposing themselves. In the end, he made the change to their asset allocation plan as they requested.

From that point on, interest rates declined steadily. By 2012, when Nathan and Karen were 70 years old, the rate for five-year CDs was only 1.25%. As rates declined, so did Nathan and Karen's income from their investments, to the point where they had to start using their principal to pay living expenses, which further reduced their income. This caused them tremendous anxiety, and for good reason, because they found themselves facing the very real possibility of running out of capital in their lifetimes. The only solution was to significantly cut their living expenses, which led to a greatly diminished standard of living.

Nathan and Karen's experience stands in stark contrast to other clients who retired in similar financial circumstances around the same time but stayed true to the wealth management journey. Many of these clients not only had sufficient income to maintain their desired lifestyle without invading principal, but they eventually saw their assets continue to grow. Instead of facing the possibility of running out of capital, they probably will outlive their money. This gives them the opportunity to do something with it, either in terms of inheritance to individuals or contributions to charity after they've passed away.

∧

Taken to its logical conclusion, the long-term approach to wealth management includes estate planning, because it's our experience that one generation's success can become the foundation of the next generation's journey. Paul and I recognize that part of our responsibility is to help our clients manage their wealth across multiple generations. We do this through the logistics of estate planning. We also educate the younger generations in the principles of long-term investing, so they are prepared to embark upon their own wealth management journey when the time comes. To that end, we make it a point to interact with clients' children whenever possible, to explain what we're doing for their parents and why we're doing it. Where we've been successful in these efforts, we've seen a remarkable consistency in the approach to investing from generation to generation, and the long-term results have been very good. In some cases, we are beginning to invest money for a third generation, and we continue with the same educational approach.

We've also had clients who weren't interested in educating their children in the principles of the wealth management journey or involving them in the process at all; in these cases we've seen very different results. When the clients eventually passed away, their children were not prepared to handle the significant amount of money they inherited.

Managing money is a learned skill; it's not something you know how to do automatically. Paul and I have worked with attorneys who did plaintiff work, and they have told us stories about winning substantial settlements for their clients, $1 million or more for people who were making $40,000 to $50,000 a year, and two years later their clients were broke because they didn't know how to handle the windfall. The same thing often happens with lottery winners, the children of wealthy parents and sometimes with people who never had significant money and then receive a large inheritance. The common factor in these cases is a lack of understanding of the fundamentals of managing wealth, which makes it difficult for people to choose the path that will keep their wealth intact over time.

We have observed cases where clients have passed away and left significant inheritances to children who don't understand important aspects of the wealth management journey. There is often an assumption on the children's part that the wealth they've inherited will somehow maintain itself regardless of their short-term financial decisions. Obviously, that doesn't happen. In fact, studies have shown that approximately 70% of family wealth disappears when it is passed down through multiple generations. The common assumption is that poor estate planning is to blame for this; but less than 3% of these failures are attributable to poor estate planning or poor investment returns. The vast majority—basically all of it—is due to poor financial decision-making on the part of the members of the inheriting generations. All too often the wealth is passed down without the knowledge and discipline necessary to continue the wealth management journey.

The clients who understand this ask us to educate their children (and sometimes even their grandchildren, when they're old enough). We work with the younger generations to illustrate the principles that helped our clients successfully build and manage their wealth, so that the children and grandchildren are well prepared to make the most of their inheritances.

On the topic of inheritances, Warren Buffett, whose personal net worth was estimated at $67 billion in September 2014, made an interesting comment in a Fortune Magazine interview almost 30 years ago. He said he planned to leave his children "enough money so that they feel they could do anything, but not so much that they could do nothing." While this approach isn't necessarily commonplace among wealthy families, it serves as a reminder that there are several factors to consider when deciding whether to leave money to children and grandchildren. Making that decision and working out the details can be very difficult, because it's rarely as simple as dividing an estate equally among one's children. Paul sometimes tells a personal story to illustrate the point:

"My own experience was with my father, my mother having

pre-deceased him. He left an estate of $200,000, which at the time wasn't a significant amount of money, particularly when it was divided among five children. You'd think it was an easy equation: five children, $200,000, they each get $40,000.

"But my father had different thoughts. He made different observations as to the needs of his children, and so he varied the amount of money that each one got. Of the five, two received $20,000, one received $40,000 and two others received $60,000. Again, it was a decision that was made by my father in his observation of what his children needed and didn't need."

In our practice we've assisted clients with inheritance decisions that run the gamut in terms of the amounts of money involved. At one end of the spectrum, Paul worked with a very successful client, Roger, who decided when his grandchildren were young that he would invest $20,000 a year for each of them. By the time Roger's grandchildren came of age, the investments he'd started for them were worth close to $1 million each. Roger consulted with Paul before he started making these gifts. Playing devil's advocate, Paul raised an objection:

"You have no idea how these children are going to turn out. What if they grow up to be goofy kids?"

"Then they'll be goofy kids with money," Roger said, "rather than goofy kids without any money."

At the other end of the spectrum was a client who had accumulated a net worth in excess of $10 million, and he made the observation that neither of his children were capable of handling any amounts of money. So, in his will, he provided for each one to receive a nominal inheritance, under $200,000; everything else went to charity. This is an extreme example, but not entirely uncommon.

∧

I led my last expedition as a professional mountain guide in the summer of 2005, but I still love to climb, and I take advantage of every opportunity I can to get out to the mountains. I love that there's always another challenge waiting—another route, another style of climbing or terrain, another level of difficulty. For me, one of those challenges is big wall climbing.

Big wall climbing is just what you'd expect from the name: climbing long routes on tall, steep mountain walls. These routes often scale thousands of feet of steep, difficult rock and can take more than a day (and sometimes weeks) to complete, making it necessary for parties to haul heavy loads of gear, food and water with them as they go. It's not uncommon for climbers on multi-day ascents to sleep in portable tents, called portaledges, lashed to the side of a sheer cliff face hundreds or even thousands of feet above the ground. By any measure—technical skill, physical and mental stamina, logistics, time—big wall climbing is a serious undertaking. The upside is that you get to test yourself on some of the world's most iconic climbing walls, such as Half Dome and El Capitan in Yosemite Valley, California.

In the summer of 2010, my climbing partner, Mike, and I set our sights on one historic big wall climb in particular: the Regular Northwest Face of Half Dome. Having completed several big wall routes together over the past few years, we wondered if we could one-up ourselves by doing the Regular Northwest Face in under 24 hours. To accomplish this, we would have to leave behind the portaledge and the haul bags with extra gear, food and water, and attempt to ascend the 2,000-foot route "fast and light" with only our skill and what we could carry in day packs.

I should stress that our goal was nothing exceptional or cutting-edge in the world of climbing. The first ascent of the Regular Northwest Face was done in 1957 by Royal Robbins and his team over the course of five days, but now most ascents are completed in two days, with just one night on the wall— and the best climbers in the world can reach the summit in a matter of hours (the record for the fastest ascent of the route is 1 hour, 22 minutes!). We weren't trying to set any records with our 24-hour goal, but for us it represented a huge leap in ambition and objective, and we knew everything would have to go perfectly if we were to be successful.

Mike and I started up the route before dawn on a brisk June morning. The northwest face of Half Dome is notoriously shady, and we found deep snow at the base of the wall, but overall the conditions looked promising. Both of us had trained for months beforehand, and we were feeling physically fit and mentally strong as we carefully made our way up the snow-covered terrain to where the route began. We had winnowed our gear to the barest essentials. We were well prepared and fully committed. Yet, as the massive granite face of Half Dome loomed overhead, I found myself grappling internally with the same questions I always faced in the moments before starting a big climb: Am I capable of this? What are all the things that could go wrong up there? I tried hard to push these thoughts out of my head and focus on our goal.

We ascended the first few pitches by headlamp as the darkness in the valley slowly brightened to daylight. The moment I touched the rock and started climbing, all my doubts fell away. The only thing in my mind was the climb itself—the next move, the next foothold, the next gear placement, the next anchor. After two hours we were 450 feet up the route and making great time (for us). We couldn't have been happier.

At this point, we had reached the fourth pitch, a section where there are a couple different ways to proceed. We spotted two British climbers taking on the difficult variation to the left of the easier line Mike and I were climbing. I was on lead for this pitch, clipping bolts and plugging gear into a right-facing flake, when the climber to my left took a bad fall. His terrified scream shattered the early morning air, and I looked up just in time to see him slam into the wall 15 feet away from me. He landed back first and upside down, and the back of his head slapped against the polished rock with a sickening thud. He wasn't wearing a helmet.

This looked like it was going to be a horrible situation. I couldn't reach the injured climber from where I was, but I could see that he was alive and somehow still conscious. I called down to Mike and the injured climber's partner, who were together on the same belay ledge, and told them to lower us both down to the ledge. Once all of us were on the ledge, Mike, who is a doctor, evaluated the climber's injuries as best he could. The climber was bleeding and disoriented, and we knew it was imperative that he get to a hospital as quickly as possible. Rather than leave him and his partner to wait for a rescue team to reach them up on the wall, Mike and I decided it would be best to tie several ropes together and lower the injured climber directly to the ground from the belay ledge. Working together with a guide who had been climbing nearby, we got the climber and his partner down quickly and safely, and a helicopter arrived a short time later to airlift him out of the valley.

After we were sure the injured climber was in good hands, Mike and I sat on the belay ledge at the base of the fourth pitch and discussed what we should do next. The rescue had taken several hours and rattled our nerves a bit. As we talked it over we discovered we were both still committed to our objective of climbing Half Dome in a day. We decided that we still had a chance to do it, even with the delay, because it was June and the days were long.

We continued climbing, pushing ourselves to the limits of our abilities until twilight overtook us 1,800 feet up the wall—tantalizingly close to the summit, but not close enough to make our objective of topping out the route in a day. We decided to bivouac for the night on a small ledge about the size of a coffee table with no tent or sleeping bags to keep us warm, just the down jackets we'd stowed in our packs. The night was shivering cold, but the next morning we woke up to beautiful clear skies above us with the valley still cast in deep shadows below—a view worth every moment of suffering. We pushed on, stiff and sore from sleeping on the bare granite ledge, and reached the summit before noon.

After we returned to our camp in the valley, Mike and I had a chance to reflect on everything that had happened. We estimated that if we'd kept up our original pace and not delayed for hours to help rescue the injured British climber, we would have completed the climb in a single day, as planned. Some people may view this experience as a missed opportunity—all the training and preparation gone to waste because of someone else's mistake—but we were proud of what we'd accomplished, both in our climbing and in our response to the emergency situation.

I grew up reading climbing stories, adventure books and harrowing tales of rescue and triumph, and found myself miffed by the occasional examples of individuals who stepped over injured or dying climbers in order to fulfill their own ambitions, indifferent to the long-term consequences of their decisions. I believe climbers have to take care of each other up high, because no one else can. In my mind, it's more meaningful to stop your climb to assist another climber than it is to push on and complete your own ascent.

Climbing has a tendency to cast the differences between short-term thinking and long-term thinking into stark relief, maybe because the consequences of making the wrong decisions are so immediate and so significant. What happened on Half Dome was another reminder of the importance of always taking the long view in life. Although Mike and I failed to accomplish our climbing goal, the experience of those two days will always be a personal triumph for me, and an example of what it means to do the right thing.

∧

CHAPTER 6
Summary Points

▸ Those who embrace the principles of the wealth management journey understand that making money is simply a means to an end, not an end in itself. The ultimate goal of the journey is to provide long-term financial security.

▸ Retirement is a common milestone of the wealth management journey. The journey doesn't end here; it simply enters another phase. At this point, the objectives of the journey often change from growth to income and asset preservation, but the same principles of a conservative, fundamentally sound approach to investing continue to apply.

▸ A typical post-retirement asset allocation plan reduces a client's exposure to equities, but won't eliminate them entirely.

▸ The long-term approach to wealth management includes estate planning. Estate planning can help one generation's success become the foundation of the next generation's wealth management journey.

▸ Managing money is a learned skill. Educating younger generations in the principles of long-term investing is a way to teach children and grandchildren this valuable skill.

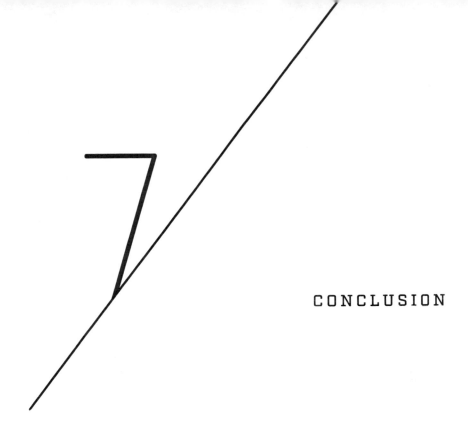

am sitting in a tent again, exhausted after back-to-back days of climbing. The air is thick with moisture and the scent of springtime in Kentucky's Red River Gorge—damp earth and ancient sandstone, dense forests awakening. It has been raining all weekend, some of the worst thunderstorms I've ever experienced. Outside my tent, heavy clouds threaten another downpour. All around me, people are hastily packing up in the hope of escaping the campground before the calm passes.

No, I haven't gone back to guiding, but this is still a familiar scene in my life—the tent, the campground, the fickle weather. My ambitions are different now, and so is the landscape. I do most of my climbing on the weekends, road trips to Kentucky or West Virginia, or wherever I can go and still make it back to the office in time for work Monday morning. This weekend it was Kentucky, and despite the near-constant rain, my partners and I made the most of our two days in the Gorge. We avoided the popular areas and the steep overhangs where the routes would be dry, choosing instead to hike through deluge in search of cliffs far off the beaten path. We bushwhacked overgrown trails, scrambled up muddy embankments and found ourselves on some of the most classic climbs in Kentucky. Conditions weren't ideal, to say the least, but the whole weekend was an adventure, and we loved every minute of it.

Closing my eyes, I try to imagine that I'm back in the Nevada desert, in the cold rain and ethereal fog. *It was raining in the desert* ... The memory is vivid but also elusive. My guiding days seem like they're from a different lifetime. Was I really leading first ascents in Alaska, high-altitude ice climbing in Bolivia and climbing crumbly desert towers in the American Southwest just ten years ago? It's hard to believe how much has changed.

Thunder rolls through the Kentucky hollers, interrupting my reverie. I start to pack up my gear. The weekend is over and it's time to head home. The Nevada desert lies 2,000 miles to the west, but I'll be driving north, to Michigan. I have client meetings tomorrow. I have a book to finish.

∧

Writing this book has been an opportunity to reflect on why I left Michigan to become a guide, and why I ultimately gave up guiding to come back. Putting these thoughts down on paper has made me realize that the emotional intensity that drove me to explore the world—and still inspires me to climb—is the same intensity that inspires in me a longing for family and familiarity, a longing to settle into a comforting state of being that we call home.

During my guiding years, I would often feel homesick when I was away from my family for long periods of time. At first, I thought this was because I didn't have a home of my own, a place to live that wasn't a tent or my Jeep. Then I heard homesickness described as an expression of love, and I knew that's what I was feeling—not a longing for a place itself, but rather, a longing for the relationships that permeate our experience of that place.

Not surprisingly, I stopped feeling homesick once I moved back to Michigan. I traded guiding and the mountains, which I still love, for the relationships that make this place home. As much as I try to always appreciate being home and having the opportunity to spend time with my family and work alongside my dad, I'm sure I sometimes take it all for granted, in the same way that I sometimes took the beauty and grandeur of the mountains for granted when I was guiding.

Fortunately, I'm often reminded of how truly special the relationships in my life are. Recently, I ran into Susan, an adult daughter of one of Paul's first and longest-tenured clients, Tommy. Tommy had passed away several years ago, after battling a difficult illness. My dad was there for Tommy and his family through it all, not just as Tommy's financial advisor, but as his friend. Susan and I crossed paths by chance on a street corner in downtown Birmingham, Michigan. It was a much-too-cold-to-stop-and-chat winter day, but she stopped to chat anyway. She wanted to compliment my father's integrity, she told me, because Paul had continued to help out even after most of Tommy's money was gone, a kindness she would never forget. "It was never about wealth for your father," she said; "it was always about relationships."

Susan was right: for Paul, everything is about relationships. On the rare occasion that a client leaves us, my dad never laments the loss of business; his disappointment comes from the loss of the relationship. It's not a kitschy throwback to the bygone days of yesteryear, when a handshake and your word were all you needed to finalize a deal. It's another one of the many lessons I'll forever be grateful for having learned from my dad: a genuine commitment to relationships, and to honoring the loyalty and history that define them. He taught me to always honor the relationship first, then focus on the specifics of the deal. And don't be surprised if friendship follows.

As I listened to Susan talk about how much she appreciated my father's integrity and his friendship with her own father, I was reminded of something my dad said during our interviews for the book. When I asked him to describe his wealth management practice in five words or fewer, he immediately replied: "Helping my friends to succeed."

He went on to explain that there are many ways to define success. "It's multifaceted," he said. "It's financial success. It's peer recognition. It's success in relationships. It's making a difference in people's lives. For me, professionally, the most important is the success of my clients, when they achieve their financial goals—goals that we worked together to fulfill over a long period of time. Where I've helped them achieve their goals, to me that's the measure of my success in this profession."

And the fact that so many clients became his friends?

"That's a more personal measure of success, and equally important," he said. "It means I made a difference in more ways than one."

Susan would have agreed.

⌃

The more things change, the more they stay the same. It's a cliché, but it's also true.

In climbing, the tools we use today are more technologically advanced than they've ever been, but they're still just axes and ropes, carabiners and warm clothing. The introduction of carbon fiber and aircraft-grade aluminum and the latest Space Age manufacturing synthetic materials in our tools hasn't changed the fundamental nature of the mountains, or of climbing itself. The risks of an avalanche or icefall are no different than they were 100 years ago, although our knowledge of the science behind these hazards has improved. We still start at the base of the mountain, and we ascend and descend using our own strength, skill and volition.

The same thing has happened with the financial markets: the tools, computers, software and investment techniques are all faster, more efficient and more sophisticated than they've ever been. Today, investors have access to more information ever before, and tomorrow they will have access to even more; the pace of change is accelerating every day. With each advancement, investors are tempted by those four dangerous words: *this time it's different*. Paul and I don't see these advancements changing the fundamentals of investing, or the fundamentals of human nature. We believe the core concepts remain the same: Investors are still driven by fear and greed. Companies still need to produce new and better products more efficiently in order to increase their earnings. The markets still move in cycles of growth and decline, volatile and unpredictable in the short term but climbing steadily over the long term. For the patient investor, the wealth management journey continues as it always has.

Is this time different? I know the answer my dad would give, and I wholeheartedly agree.

ABOUT THE AUTHOR

Jay Hack is a Certified Financial Planner® in partnership with his dad, Paul, at Hack Wealth Management of Raymond James in Farmington Hills, Michigan; together they manage client portfolios in excess of $300 million. Before he became a financial advisor, Jay was a mountain guide for the American Alpine Institute. Among his many adventures, he guided clients to the summit of Mt. McKinley, led first ascents of other peaks in Alaska and climbed volcanoes in Ecuador. As a guide, his client list included C-suite executives of Fortune 500 companies, U.S. military personnel and seasoned climbers. His proudest personal achievements in climbing include the *Supercouloir* on Mt. Blanc Du Tacul in the French Alps; *Repentance* in New Hampshire; and big wall routes in Yosemite National Park. Jay holds an MBA from the Kogod School of Business at American University in Washington, D.C., where he was the commencement speaker for his graduating class along with former Federal Reserve Chair Paul Volker. He sits on the executive board of the Anti-Defamation League and the board of Orchards Children's Services, and he was the President of NEXTGen Detroit. He lives in Detroit with his wife.

A NOTE ON THE TYPE

This book was set in the typeface Surveyor, by Hoefler & Co. Known by its designers as "a mapmaker's letter," Surveyor's proportions and serifs mimic the characteristic letterforms of traditional copperplate cartography engravings of the early 19th century. Maps in those times embodied the essence of adventure and discovery, at once tools of the explorer's trade and artifacts of its practice. By capturing that spirit of adventure, Surveyor nods to explorers both then and now.